Mastering *the* Methods

D.V. Hurst

Dwayne Turner

Gospel Publishing House
Springfield, Missouri
02-0340

5th Printing 2004

Printed in the United States of America

ISBN: 0-88243-085-8

Contents

Introduction

The success of a teacher is in direct proportion to the amount of learning that takes place within his or her classroom. It is imperative, then, for the teacher to do whatever it takes to facilitate the learning process.

Mastering the Methods is designed to help teachers maximize their opportunities in the classroom. Understanding that the students in any classroom represent a variety of learning styles, the authors of this book present a variety of methods that will help teachers relate to each of their students.

Active, involved, and creative teaching methods for teachers of every age-level are the focus of this fundamental training book. Answers to why, when, and how to use these methods are also provided.

It is our hope that you will find the principles related in this book to be insightful and easy to implement.

* 1 *

The Master Teacher

Jesus must have been a compelling teacher to cause the temple guards to disobey their orders.

The guards had been sent to take Him. The Pharisees and chief priests had heard the murmurings of the Jews. Many had believed on Jesus and reasoned, " 'When the Christ comes, will he do more miraculous signs than this man?' " Out of deep concern, therefore, the chief priests issued the orders. But Jesus was teaching, so the officers listened. His words carried weight and He spoke with authority. Division concerning Him arose among the people, "but no one laid a hand on him."

When the officers returned without Him and the Pharisees and chief priests asked, " 'Why didn't you bring him in?' " the guards only defense was, " 'no one ever spoke the way this man does.' "

In _who He was_, _what He taught_, _how He taught_, and _why He taught_, Jesus is the Christian teacher's example. With a probing question, a startling statement, a meaningful parable, a thoughtful lecture, a look of understanding and compassion, a word of revelation, or a challenging command, Jesus led people out of failure and sin into new life, joy, and peace.

Contrast has been drawn between the teaching of Jesus and that of the typical rabbi of His day. When progressing beyond the teaching of the rabbi to that of Jesus, "the transition is like passing out of an old dusty attic that has not been aired for months, into the clear crisp atmosphere of a bright spring morning."[1]

Such a fresh and invigorating experience reflects not only the content of the teaching but also the methods used. It also hints at the supreme quality of the Teacher himself, a teacher who is better contrasted with His contemporaries than compared.

Distinction has also been drawn between the method and teaching of Socrates and that of Jesus. "Socrates," it is said, "asked questions which his disciples tried to answer; Jesus provoked His disciples to ask questions which He answered."[2] The basic difference in the approach of the two is clearly in evidence. The one assumed man could find the answers; the other knew ultimate answers came only from God. But, despite this, Jesus sought to stir the thinking, to set the minds of His students in ferment, so that they would learn. He then encouraged them to learn of Him.

Every Christian teacher must enroll in Jesus's class and learn of Him—of His person in all His wonder and glory, His position as a teacher, His message, His method, and His motive. As H. H. Horne has suggested, "Our methods of moral and religious education will not be perfected until we have sat at the feet of Jesus the Master Teacher." If one would obey Christ's commission and teach, he would first do well to study Jesus the Teacher.

In this survey of the Master Teacher, therefore, we shall consider the Man, His message, His method, and His motive.

8

The Man

Jesus was more than a teacher, much more. He was declared to be the Son of God, the Savior of the world, the self-sacrificing High Priest, the Lord. But He was also a teacher. C. H. Benson declared that "of the ninety times our Lord was addressed in the gospel record, sixty times He was called rabbi or teacher."[4] From His associates and contemporaries as well as from His own lips testimony can be derived and that conclusion reached:

1. *Jesus considered himself a teacher.* Everywhere in the Gospel record evidence is found that Jesus regarded himself as a teacher. Repeatedly the writers declare, "He taught in their synagogues" and elsewhere (Matthew 4:23; 9:35; Mark 1:21; 6:2; Luke 4:15; 6:6; 13:10; John 6:59). In a wide variety of circumstances and settings, His constant response was to teach.

The final evidence that Jesus was a teacher is found in His own direct statement: " 'You call me "Teacher" and "Lord," and rightly so, for that is what I am' " (John 13:13). Jesus welcomed the title Teacher. Thus, in act and in word it is evident He regarded himself as a teacher.

2. *His disciples considered Him a teacher.* They seldom addressed Him in any other way. When threatened by the storms they cried, " 'Teacher, don't you care if we drown' " (Mark 4:38). When confused by the teaching regarding the destruction of the temple they asked, " 'Teacher, . . . when will these things happen?' " (Luke 21:7). Even Judas, under extreme pressure at the Last Supper knowing he was to betray Jesus, said, " 'Surely not I, Rabbi?' " (Matthew 26:25). When desiring to learn to pray, although they addressed Him as Lord, they did implore, " 'Teach us to pray' " (Luke 11:1). It was most natural for them to address Him as teacher, for thus they regarded Him.

9

3. *Others considered Him a teacher.* Nicodemus's statement, " 'Rabbi, we know you are a teacher who has come from God,' " is well known (John 3:2). ("Rabbi" is the Hebrew designation for teacher.) The rich young ruler called Him " 'Teacher' " (Matthew 19:16). The Pharisees and Herodians addressed Him likewise, " 'Teacher, we know you are a man of integrity . . . You teach the way of God in accordance with the truth' " (Mark 12:14; see also Matthew 22:24,36; Mark 9:17; 12:32; Luke 12:13; 19:39). After hearing His instruction, the scribe said, " 'Well said, teacher, . . . you are right' "(Mark 12:32).

4. *He possessed great authority as a teacher.* His credentials were himself, His message, truth. He possessed the highest moral and intellectual qualifications. He needed no letters of authority. He was introduced by no other than the Father himself and by John the Baptist. From then on He was on the stage, as it were, and taught, being "glorified" of many.

Once in the temple the chief priests and scribes challenged His authority. He met them by asking if the source of John the Baptist's authority was, "from heaven or from men?" He hung them in a dilemma, and they could not answer. He responded by saying, " 'Neither will I tell you by what authority I am doing these things' " (Luke 20:8).

As McKoy has said, "Rabbinical authority could add nothing to a commission from the most High. Jesus felt that the prophetic spirit stirring within Him was all the authority that He needed."[5] It was true of Him even as He said to His own disciples, " 'It will not be you speaking, but the Spirit of your Father speaking through you'. " (Matthew 10:20).

His Message

The soldiers said, " 'No one ever spoke the way this man does.' " The comparison was broad, including what He said. The things Jesus taught were new, fresh, and filled with life. His message can be approached from varying points of view. For example, it can be said that His was a message from the Father to individuals:

❧ 1. *From the Father*—The source of His message was well documented. At the Transfiguration the Father announced, " 'This is my Son, whom I love; with him I am well pleased. Listen to him!' " (Matthew 17:5). Jesus himself said, " 'The words I say to you are not just my own. Rather, it is the Father, living in me, who is doing his work' " (John 14:10). And earlier He said, " 'The very work that the Father has given me to finish, and which I am doing, testifies that the Father has sent me' " (John 5:36). Jesus's message was from God, the Father; truly He had "heard from heaven."

❧ 2. *To individuals*—The goal of His message was evident in both what He said and what He did. H. H. Horne says, "Jesus began with individuals, continued with crowds, and ended with individuals, during three successive main periods of His ministry."[6]

On many occasions, Jesus was seen teaching large crowds and multitudes totaling even 4,000 and 5,000, extremely large crowds for that day. On other occasions, He was seen teaching small groups. It was not the crowd to which Jesus came; but to the individual persons in the crowd. He always spoke person to person.

Another approach to Jesus's message can be taken in identifying the main topics that concerned Him. W. Sanday notes several distinct and characteristic topics: "The Fatherhood of God, the Kingdom of God, the subjects and members of the Kingdom, the Messiah, the Paraclete, and the Trinity of God."[7] In studying the Gospels, one sees these topics recurring again and again.

11

A third approach to Christ's message can be seen in His teaching concerning relationships between God and all humankind and between individuals. In talking of people's relationship to God, Jesus dealt with the past, the present, and the future:

1. *The past*—He said, " 'I have not come to abolish, but to fulfill' " (Matthew 5:17). In fulfilling the Law, Jesus confirmed and sealed God's previous relationship with man.

2. *The present*—His was a message of present personal relationship to God through Him—" 'Come to me' " (Matthew 11:28).

3. *The future*—He said, " 'I will come back and take you to be with me that you also may be where I am' " (John 14:3).

His teaching concerning interpersonal relationships touched on both those within the fellowship of believers and those outside the fellowship. (Later, the teachings were extended in the epistles.) In many of His parables He laid down principles of relationship. Also, some of them were given in response to questions and in His more lengthy discourses. His teaching encompassed all areas of society.

Still a fourth approach to Jesus's message can be taken in considering His central themes. Over and over love appears as an underlying cardinal theme—" 'Love the Lord your God . . . [and] love your neighbor' " (Matthew 22:37,39). How often ethical teachings must return to Jesus's basic premises to find foundation for teaching or to sum up the matter.

Five essential qualifications of a world-class teacher are suggested by H. H. Horne: (1) a vision that encompasses the world, (2) knowledge of the heart of man, (3) mastery of the subject taught, (4) aptness in teaching, and (5) a life that embodies the teaching.[8]

It can be conclusively shown that each of these was never

more true of anyone than Christ. While each qualification is striking, the last stands out above them all—*a life that embodies the teaching*. Jesus said, " 'I am . . . the truth' " (John 14:6). And John said of Him, "The Word was made flesh . . . and made his dwelling among us" (John 1:14). So the Master Teacher stood out from all other teachers before and since. In an absolutely unique way, all that He said was backed up by what He was and what He did.

His Method

Jesus the Master Teacher was different not only in *what* He taught, but also in *how* He taught. His purposes, principles, and methods were in marked contrast with those of His contemporaries. His teaching exhibited variety and expertise. He taught with naturalness. This is especially evident when considered from the viewpoint of the human learning process. It was easy to learn when Jesus taught.

Whether or not Jesus was consciously aware of His artful use of methods, and whether or not He purposely employed methods as He did, cannot be determined conclusively. Nevertheless, He skillfully employed teaching methods that are still in use today. And He did so in such a masterful manner that His teaching still stands as the best example of "how to do it."

Where did Jesus learn to teach? Not from His contemporaries—the schools of Athens, Alexandria, or Rome. He studied the prophets and knew the Old Testament Scriptures well, imbibing their methodology. He observed people. He knew the workings of the human mind and how to cause people to learn. He was filled with the Spirit, himself a teacher. Finally, the very nature of His message had much to do with the way Jesus taught. His message, methods, and life were all a part of divine revelation. There existed in Him a triunity of the three. He embodied the ultimate method.

His Aim

Jesus's central purpose, or aim, in teaching was to communicate a new life and relationship to God. He said, " 'I have come that they may have life, and have it to the full' " (John 10:10). He taught that this new life and relationship are a result of two things: a spiritual *new birth* and spiritual *growth*. His further purposes in teaching included (1) instilling a new sense of values and ideals, (2) revealing people's duty to God, (3) revealing people's duty to others, (4) revealing people's duty to themselves, (5) teaching the need of faith in God, (6) presenting himself as the source of this new life and the means of relationship to God, and (7) motivating perpetuation.

As a teacher, Jesus's purposes seemed always clearly before Him. He did not deal in nonessentials, vague philosophies, or the periphery of life. He dealt with *the* questions of life.

Teaching Principles

Jesus based His teaching on sound teaching principles and learning laws. He knew how to work with the minds of others and did what was necessary to facilitate learning. Notice, for example, the following:

1. *Jesus knew the value of winning and holding attention.* He called for it—"Behold." He used challenging statements, questions, stories, visuals, objects, and imagery. He painted word pictures and taught in terms His listeners could understand.

2. *Jesus sought to establish a point of contact.* He related what He taught to what was uppermost in His listeners' minds.

3. *Jesus related His teaching to what was already known—the law*

14

of apperception. It is the principle of teaching the unknown by means of the known. It is learning through comparison and contrast or through showing similarities. The key question is often asked by the learner trying to understand, "What is it like?"

4. *Jesus encouraged student participation and activity*. His students were not just spectators. He knew that to learn, students must think and act for themselves. The common response in learning, "Let me try!" is significant here. The words *come, go, follow, do*, and *preach,* were used repeatedly by Jesus. He fully recognized the need for learning by doing.

5. *Jesus recognized the relation of impression to expression in learning*. His classroom was often a laboratory, and sometimes He employed the field trip. Thus, He enforced the principle for His disciples, His more advanced students.

6. *Jesus sought always to motivate His students*. Motivation is the why of learning. He recognized the importance of motivation and sought to release, not just temporary, but lasting and continuous motives in His students:

  a. He based His motivation on a revelation of divine truth, appealing not only to emotion, but also to intellect and will, understanding and duty.

  b. He appealed to the intrinsic motive, love.

  c. He used some extrinsic motivations, benefits and rewards.

  d. He appealed to conscience as a motivating factor.

  e. He taught that the Holy Spirit would provide motivation—He would guide into truth.

l Various Methods Jesus Employed

The teaching methods Jesus used are basic to all good teaching. Without the aid of all sorts of electronic, visual, mechanical, and other devices, Jesus was able to communicate by word of mouth, one to one, in such a way that the world still remembers what He taught. Surely there is great value in the use of the basic methods:

* 1. *Question and answer*—H. H. Horne suggests that here "we are near the heart of the teaching methods of Jesus," and notes that the Gospels record over 100 of His questions. At the age of twelve, Jesus was "asking them questions" (Luke 2:46). Early in His ministry He probed Andrew and John's purpose, " 'What do you want?' " (John 1:38). His second recorded query was to Nathanael, "Because I said unto thee, I saw thee under the fig tree, believest thou?" (John 1:50, KJV). His third recorded question was to His mother, " 'Dear woman, why do you involve me?' " (John 2:4). Each of these provocative questions gives hints as to Jesus's future use of the question method.

* 2. *Discussion*—Jesus used the informal conversational discussion method often. Some of His most significant revelations came at such times. Prominent in His conversational teaching experiences were (a) the woman of Samaria (John 4); (b) Nicodemus, the Pharisee (John 3:1–21); (c) the rich young ruler (Matthew 19:16–30); and (d) Simon, the Pharisee (Luke 7:36–50).

* 3. *Lecture*—Jesus also very skillfully employed the lecture method, using it in both large and small crowds. Sometimes His lecture was long; other times it was short. The subjects ranged from wealth and divorce to Sabbath

16

and missions. At least sixty of Jesus's lectures are found in the Gospels. Some of the more prominent ones are (a) His farewell message in John 14 through 17 (His longest); (b) the Sermon on the Mount (Matthew 5 through 7); and (c) His discourse on judgment and the end times (Matthew 24 and 25).

4. *Stories and parables*—Jesus used the story method more than any other. His parables are known the world over. He has been called the world's greatest storyteller. His sixty-one parables may be categorized as follows: (a) of things, sixteen; (b) of plants, two; (c) of animals, four; and (d) of human beings, thirty-four. The emphasis was on the human. Some famous parables are The Lost Coin, The Unprofitable Servant, The Good Samaritan, The Ten Virgins, and The Foolish Rich Man.

5. *Teaching aids*—In a very natural way, Jesus used teaching aids:

   a. Illustrations—The wind to illustrate the Holy Spirit and the small mustard seed to illustrate faith are well known.

   b. Objects and demonstrations—The little child in the midst and bread are examples, as well as the washing of the disciples' feet.

   c. Visual aids—The normal settings and sounds of life were His audiovisuals. Wherever Jesus was, real life formed His flannelboard, chalkboard, and video equipment.

His Motive

J. B. Tidwell says, "Of all the power of Jesus, His heart power was most effective."[9] Without doubt it can be said that Jesus was the most motivated man who ever lived:

⮡ 1. *Jesus was motivated out of obedience.* " 'My food,' said Jesus, 'is to do the will of him who sent me and to finish his work' " (John 4:34). Certainly, the love existent within the Godhead precipitated this obedience, for Jesus linked the two, " 'If you love me, you will obey what I command' " (John 14:15).

◖ 2. *Jesus was motivated by love, love for the Father and for those whom the Father loved ("For God so loved . . .").* This love for His students was so evident in Christ's teaching, when He "looked at Peter," when He prayed for them, and when He patiently taught them, recognizing their weaknesses. It was seen when He wept over Jerusalem and when He saw the multitude and was moved with compassion. It was finally seen when He gave His life for His disciples and His enemies. " 'Greater love has no one than this, that he lay down his life for his friends' " (John 15:13). A Christian teacher shows love for the students, and for all people.

❋ ❋ ❋ ❋

Endnotes

1. Charles Francis McKoy, *The Art of Jesus as a Teacher* (Philadelphia: The Judson Press, 1930), 33.

2. James Stalker, *Imago Christi* (New York: American Tract Society, 1880), 269.

3. H. H. Home, *Jesus the Master Teacher* (Grand Rapids: Kregel Publications, 1964), 1.

4. C. H. Benson, *History of Christian Education* (Chicago: Moody Press, 1943), 34.

5. McKoy, *The Art of Jesus as a Teacher,* 28.

6. H. H. Home, *Jesus the Master Teacher,* 142.

7. W. Sanday, "Jesus Christ," *A Dictionary of the Bible,* ed. James Hastings (New York: Charles Scribner's Sons, 1899, vol. 2), 618.

8. H. H. Horne, *Jesus the Master Teacher,* 184.

9. J. B. Tidwell, *The Sunday School Teacher Magnified* (Westwood, N.J.: Fleming H. Revell Company, 1918), 32.

✳ 2 ✳

Understanding Your Students and Meeting Their Needs

As far back as 1884, John Gregory stated a law of teaching that still applies: "The language used in teaching must be common to teacher and learner." He amplified the law to the effect that the "words must be understood by each, with the same meaning to both."[1]

Inherent in the law is the principle that if a teacher is to relate to students and teach them in words they can understand and receive, the teacher must *know* the students. Teachers should know their students as *representative* of others their age and they should know them *personally* with each one's individual differences. The teacher must see students as developing people who are changing and maturing, and understand them as they are now.

Getting To Know the Students

There are ways to know the students, their characteristics, their needs, and their developing personalities:

1. *The prospective teachers should decide which age-level students*

21

they would like to teach, based on their own interests and natural aptitudes. The prospective teachers should then study materials written about that stage in life's development. (They should first study the appropriate age-level handbook available from Gospel Publishing House.)[2] In their studies, the teachers will become aware of the characteristics, needs, ways of working with the particular age-group, and special challenges they will face.

→ [P] *2. The teachers should study the members of the classes to which they are assigned.* They will want to know them as a group, learning how they relate to one another, how they respond, what they have done together, and any special problems or successes that may be evident in the group.

→ [*] *3. The teachers should get to know each student personally as quickly as possible.* Nothing can replace a personal relationship and rapport with each student. Jesus spent much time cultivating that special rapport with His students. To those to whom He would later entrust so much in sacred mission, His disciples, He related personally in years of giving of himself to them and learning to know them. Then He could teach them, both as persons and as a cooperating group.

If prospective teachers study the handbook for their chosen age-level and then together discuss the developing students, the teachers will gain a greater sense of the task. Understanding the students' characteristics and needs before class, while they are in the class, and after they leave will give teachers a more realistic perspective.

[*] The following brief summation of age-level characteristics and educational implications growing out of them can serve as a guideline in this discussion and as a means of review.

Characteristics

Physical

Rapid growth; active; tire soon; senses of taste and touch are especially eager for stimulation; unable to sing in tune

Mental

Learning through repetition; learning with five senses; limited but growing vocabulary; attention span, two to five minutes; learn by seeing and doing

Emotional

Dependent; timid; have imaginary fears; sensitive to atmosphere; need security and attention; become upset when tired; seek adult attention

Social

Self-centered; trustful; loving, need love; anger at frustration; happy; little group feeling; likes to play alone beside another student

Spiritual

See God as real and living; pray readily; can love God readily; imitators; can think of Jesus as best friend; Bible can be special

Implications

Variety needed; move from activity to activity in class. Give them things to feel and handle. Let them look, feel, smell, and linger. Use stories into which they can "enter," and pictures and objects they can handle and "fill in." Avoid symbolism; use simple, short learning activities.

Teach them to share, to love and trust God, the teacher, and others. Provide many opportunities for self-expression, guided expression; make Sunday School a pleasant experience. Teach them to pray, sing, and worship. Encourage them to express love. Repeat a few easy-to-grasp Bible verses often.

Provide individual attention. Talk in a quiet voice and be calm. Avoid confusion. Make them feel at home. When possible include teachers of both genders. Vary activities to include large muscles and quiet activities. Lead the children to discover God.

FOUR- AND FIVE-YEAR-OLD CHILDREN

Physical

Rapid growth; muscle development; lacking fine coordination; adept in certain play skills; aggressive players; tire easily

Mental

Curious; have short attention span, four to eight minutes; vivid imaginations, and limited vocabulary; literalism; imitators who learn by doing

Emotional

Excitement; beginning to develop sympathy for others

Social

Self-centered; friendly; imitative; want approval; seek group play opportunities

Spiritual

Eager to learn about God; trust and love God; can differentiate between right and wrong; can experience real worship, believe

Implications

Provide activity time in class session. Give them some responsibility. Vary the class session.

Answer and use their questions. Provide variety; use imagination (e.g., role playing and stories). Give simple, clear

24

directions; use words they know. Don't assume children remember from previous weeks.

Teach them to share. Provide a good example. Befriend them and show love. You may have to deal with jealousy and anger.

Teach God's love; guide expression. Teach them to relate to God in prayer and to know God approves biblically sound behavior. Provide worship time; teach them to experience Jesus's presence.

SIX- AND SEVEN-YEAR-OLD CHILDREN

Physical
Irregular growth; active, want to "do"

Mental
Attention span, six to eight minutes; literal-minded, think concretely; imaginative; reasoning; credulous; interested in physical needs; have many questions

Emotional
Happy; excitable; impatient; need security; sympathetic; can express love

Social
Friendly to their own age-group; selfish; like to help; need self-expression; prefer individual activity; need adult approval

Spiritual
Have natural faith and believe in prayer; respond spiritually; usually like Sunday School; discriminators; see God as loving, holy, and strong; know Jesus changes lives

Implications
Provide active times. Provide opportunities for them to express themselves.

Vary procedures. Be clear and precise. Help them distinguish between real and unreal. Reason with them; never belittle them. Take their questions seriously.

Stay calm and enjoy class. Teach patience and confidence in God. Encourage them to empathize with others' needs.

Group them together, and teach them to share. Provide tasks—things they can do to help. Guide self-expression; express love and friendship.

Provide worship and prayer times. Encourage them to respond to Christ and to experience His help and love. Emphasize God's greatness. Give regular opportunities to accept Christ.

EIGHT- AND NINE-YEAR-OLD CHILDREN

Physical

Have refined eye-hand coordination; are still developing some large muscles

Mental

Increased understanding of right and wrong; have an expanding concept of time, space, and distance; memorize well; enjoy art and drama; increasing reasoning power

Emotional

Usually outgoing or friendly; moods and attitudes change quickly; are worriers

Social

Want to be accepted by the peer group; are concerned about fair play, cooperation, and respect; need to become involved in meaningful church activities

Spiritual

Want to make decisions; are becoming aware of their need to accept Christ; need to know God loves them all the time; this is the time to introduce teaching about baptism in the Holy Spirit

Implications

Provide activities that permit the use of eye-hand skills. Structure activities that permit movement. Avoid having students sit for long periods of time.

Accept them for who they are. Do not be critical or lose your temper. Express sincere praise for work well done. Help them reason through questions of right and wrong.

Find ways to involve them in group projects. Encourage the development of friendships. Give students input about activities, decorations, etc. Make sure class rules are fair and enforced.

Emphasize Bible memorization; frequently employ question-and-answer games. Use maps, timelines, role plays, skits, and plays to teach and reinforce Bible lessons. Provide frequent opportunities for students to accept Christ as Savior.

TEN- AND ELEVEN-YEAR-OLD CHILDREN

Physical

Energetic and active; very well-coordinated; rovers; endurance

Mental

Power to concentrate and reason; inquisitive, eager to know; good memory; like to collect; love stories; are idealistic; enthusiastic; are able to apply biblical principles to life

Emotional

Have well-balanced emotions at age ten, but may change significantly at age eleven; have deep feelings of love and appreciation for God; have few fears, but like to experience fear vicariously; quick tempered; mixed feelings; object to display of affection; tendency to strong hatred; enjoy humor (everything is funny)

Social

Want to be part of the peer group; still associate largely with children of the same sex; are hero-worshipers

Spiritual

Ready for salvation; simple faith; habits of prayer and Bible reading; will set high standards; can grow spiritually; concerned about others' spiritual needs; can see God as Great Judge

Implications

Structure class time to allow movement. Provide a variety of activities. Provide small detailed projects such as drawing, painting, or write-on slides.

Reason with them. Encourage them to think, to memorize, and to channel interests.

Encourage group feeling and doing things together. Teach discrimination in actions and relationships.

Lead them to Christ and teach them to trust God. Set Bible study goals and encourage them to set spiritual goals. Teach them to evaluate. Emphasize missions.

Use hero stories. Be a guide, not a dictator. Make them feel they belong without physical display. Help them learn to control feelings. Laugh with them when appropriate.

TWELVE- TO FOURTEEN-YEAR-OLD STUDENTS

Physical

Change and growth (girls more quickly); complexion problems; voice changes; sexual awareness; some clumsiness

Mental

Growing ability to reason, question, and make choices; memory improves; imagination gains vividness (daydreams); self-conscious; quick judgments; eager for answers, but may appear indifferent

28

Emotional
Unpredictable, moody, and changeable; lonely; desire freedom; feel misunderstood; rebellious; frank

Social
Peer group is very important; desire for social approval; strong companionships develop; love to tease

Spiritual
Growth in capacity to respond spiritually, crucial time, honest questions, opportune time for conversion, open to baptism in the Holy Spirit

Implications
Physical activity should be part of the total curriculum. Promote self-understanding in lessons and a Christian view of sacred facts of life.

Discuss and emphasize careful thinking and values. Move from rote memory to concept retention. Help them begin to set goals.

Understanding and steadiness are needed above all else in the teacher. Provide acceptance, tactful guidance, and friendliness toward all.

Promote wholesome weekday activities and right attitudes in relationships. Foster teamwork, cooperation, and helpfulness.

Encourage personal involvement in worship and making Christ the controlling center of life and the answer in working out practical daily Christian living. Encourage them to receive the Holy Spirit in fullness.

FIFTEEN- TO SEVENTEEN-YEAR-OLD STUDENTS

Physical
Changes of adolescence; outgrowing awkwardness; maturation; two extremes—tireless to sleeping around the clock; active

Mental
Active and inquiring; reasoning; argumentation, debate;

remember ideas; creative; idealistic; independent; often doubt; want to test

Emotional

Romantic; changeable; emotional upsets

Social

Attracted to opposite sex; dating problems; standards; want help; resent "preaching"; rebel against authority; imitative, sometimes go in cliques

Spiritual

Question and doubt; faith tested in education; long for security; capable of ardent Christian living and strong growth and Christian witness

Implications

Provide opportunity for weekday activities. Offer understanding.

Provide thoughtful, creative teaching and opportunities for discussion, to express and do, to see all sides of issues, and to think and decide. Increase responsibility.

Promote Christian principles in self-understanding, in personal development, and in relating to others. Present Christ as their helper in working out daily victorious living.

Provide opportunities for wholesome association. Be a friend who can be trusted.

Demonstrate biblical principles and a personal Christianity that works. Help them discover the Word is true and Christ is real. Provide opportunities for evangelistic action.

EIGHTEEN- TO TWENTY-FOUR-YEAR-OLD STUDENTS

Physical

Reaching adulthood; increased energy; time of achievement

Mental

Reasoning fully developed; great decision time and commitments made; mental independence; much learning; creative

Emotional

Approaching maturity and more stability; less fearful and worried; concerned about love, marriage, and sex

Social

Broadening and deepening their relationships; search for life's companions; some are married; parenthood; responsibility

Spiritual

Capable of greatest growth; establishing life's patterns; time of tests

Implications

Adults enjoy and profit from discussions and Bible studies. Discuss principles for decisions. Challenge them to find God's plan for their lives.

Provide opportunities to serve and to meet and make friends (e.g., young marrieds classes). Instruct in home building, marriage relationship, and parental responsibilities.

Encourage them to make decisions on Christian principles and to pursue spiritual things. Encourage them to develop a firm faith and experience with the Word, and a Christian view of life and the world.

TWENTY-FIVE AND OLDER STUDENTS

Physical

Time of maturity; time of height and fall from physical vigor

Mental

Time of greatest productivity; can keep learning

Emotional

Time of maturity; of full, blossomed-out life; made serious by responsibility

Social

Friendships are stable; strong ambition and willpower

Spiritual

Time of keenest insight

Implications

In all respects, adulthood is the time of maturity. Full responsibilities for the class (its learning goals and activities) should be assumed by the students. Provide strong, relevant biblical teaching. Encourage them to search the Scriptures for guiding principles to life and values for setting priorities. Provide opportunities for responsible meaningful Christian service.

The use of key characteristics in the preceding listing has both value and a problem. The value is the ease of reference and guide to understanding that is inherent in identifying students' characteristics at each age-level. The problem is the tendency to oversimplify or to categorize the understanding of students in a given bracket.

It should be remembered that students are growing and developing, learning and maturing on a continuing basis, especially in the early years. At hardly any point do they really plateau.

It should also be remembered that learners are individuals with their own unique personalities. They will grow and develop in their own ways; they will respond to challenges and opportunities in unique ways; they will meet their needs and, in turn, give and serve in their own ways. The teachers must learn to know their students, therefore, as they are.[3] Nothing will accomplish that like constant association with the students through the week and in various circumstances and settings. It hardly seems teachers can learn to know their students too well!

Endnotes

1. John Gregory, *The Seven Laws of Teaching* (Grand Rapids: Baker Book House, 1954), 42.

2. *Focus on Early Childhood, Focus on Children, Focus on Youth, Focus on Adults, and Focus on Administration* are available from Gospel Publishing House. (See the Sunday School Staff Training section of the general catalog. To order call 1-800-641-4310 or write Gospel Publishing House, 1445 N. Boonville Avenue, Springfield, MO 65802-1894.)

3. Adult students now include singles, young married people, divorced people, middle-aged people, and senior citizens. Each stage faces unique challenges. It is important to recognize and stay in touch with their ever-chaning needs. The most important thing to remember about this group is that they can (and want to) add to the teaching-learning experience by bringing their own life experiences into the classroom. This can truly be a time of learning from one another.

3

Learning and Motivation

The ultimate success of teaching is measured in the learning that is done by each of the students and by the teacher. But what is learning? What factors affect the learning process? Can any principles or laws be set forth as guidelines? How does one stimulate or motivate learning? What can be done to increase the efficiency of the classroom, the more formal learning situation? These questions require the attention of the beginning teacher and the experienced teacher as well.

Motivating learning is not simple. The problem surfaces immediately when one tries to define what a teacher is or does. Some may say the teacher "shares, imparts, or transmits" knowledge. But is that adequate? Some may think so. More appropriately, however, teachers are the ones who stimulate the desire to learn and guide in the learning process, who also learn as they teach, and who know (and hope) that their students eventually will learn even more than they.

To understand the motivation of learning, at least in part, we shall analyze the two sides of the task and then attempt to synthesize them:

1. What is learning and how is it done?
2. What is motivation and how is it done?

Learning

Learning is complex. Its complexity grows out of the learner's nature and the subject matter to be learned. Many factors affect learning from the point of view of the learner: physical and psychological makeup, native ability, background, age, wants and desires, and likes and dislikes. Individual differences show up in the learning process as much as anywhere in life. The kinds of material to be learned also affect the process. For example, involved concepts versus a list of items, nonsense material versus meaningful material, interesting versus non-interesting material.

Learning has been defined differently, reflecting various theories. One definition is "growth, modification of experience, adjustment to environment, and change in behavior." It refers to the *effects of* experience on subsequent behavior.

Learning has also been defined as the "acquisition of knowledge or skill." The acquisition of knowledge is at the foundation of learning and is primarily intellectual, while the acquisition of skill is often largely physical, although based on knowledge. Learning also includes the acquisition or development of ideals, attitudes, values, and appreciations. However, they are secondary to the acquisition of knowledge, in that they result from knowledge.

The whole person is involved in learning—the intellects, sensibilities (emotions), and will. While the acquisition of ideas, for example, may often appear primarily intellectual, the learner feels something about those ideas and decides something about them. Those feelings and decisions have much to do with the behavioral changes resulting from learning and, therefore, are very much a part of the whole act of learning. Thus, what a student *knows, feels,* and *does* are the total of learning. This whole concept becomes most meaningful in religious education in that forming attitudes and making decisions are very much a part of it.

It is important, if the teacher wants students to be successful in learning, that the teacher understands the process of learning. L. O. Richards has identified the following five levels of learning, beginning with the simple and moving to the most complex kinds of learning. Studying these levels will prove beneficial to the teacher:

1. *Rote*—The most basic level of learning occurs when students are able to repeat what they have been taught, yet without independent thought of meaning. The alphabet and multiplication tables are learned, for the most part, at this level. Although there is some place for this type of learning in the Sunday School classroom, such learning has little potential for changing lives and helping Christians mature.

2. *Recognition*—The second level of learning comes when students can recognize biblical concepts that have been taught. Mastery at this level can be determined by successful completion of multiple-choice tests. This level of learning is also evident when a student says, "I've heard that Bible story before," but cannot paraphrase the story. Recognition is the second step along the way to complete, life-changing learning.

3. *Restatement*—The third level of learning takes place when students can paraphrase what they have been taught. This is evidence of independent assimilation and understanding, and represents an important step up on the stairway of learning. It shows the students can break the information into smaller parts and reassemble them in a new, yet logical way.

4. *Relation*—The fourth level of learning is evidenced by the ability to relate the biblical truth learned to the appropriate

response. Case studies are an excellent way to encourage this type of learning. Students demonstrate they can analyze the problem and relate biblical truths to it to find an appropriate solution.

5. *Realization*—The ultimate level of learning occurs when students are able to take the truth they have learned and apply it in a meaningful way to their own daily lives. Christian educators teach for life-change, and only at this fifth level can that occur.

It is important for teachers to be aware of the five levels of learning so that they will strive to facilitate many different types of learning. Learning is incomplete if the students master only the first one or two levels during a lesson. Strive to help them understand and personalize what you teach, according to their age level.

Three factors significantly affect the learning process: (1) original nature, (2) environment, and (3) purpose. The relative effect of the first two has often been debated, especially in circles where humans are looked on simply as having evolved as the highest physical being. The third factor adds spiritual overtone to the discussion and accounts for man's higher nature. Teachers should be familiar with basic information about all three factors:

1. *Original nature or heredity*—By original nature we mean the essential character or the abilities, potentialities, possibilities, tendencies, desires, and drives with which each human being enters the world. Humans are not fully developed at birth but tend to develop as they grow and mature. Original nature, then, is what one is intrinsically, before environment exerts its influence.

2. *Environment*—By environment we mean all the external factors that tend to influence development after life has begun. Whatever one contacts and responds to is a part of environment, whether in the classroom, in the home, or elsewhere. It may be separated into four groupings: physical, psychological, social, and spiritual. Each greatly affects the individual.

In comparing heredity and environment, it can be said that heredity provides the native ability and tendency, and environment provides the opportunity for the tendency to develop. It is very evident that environment greatly affects the tendency. Thus, environment is important to the teacher. The teacher is a part of it, and through it, seeks to stimulate and guide the learning process.

3. *Purpose*—Intelligent—even spiritual—purpose is one of humankind's distinguishing characteristics. Although people are physical, they are not primarily physical. They are primarily spiritual and dwell in a temples of "clay." They have the power of choice and intelligent purpose. Their development is meaningful, and their learning can be aimed at goals, even spiritual ones.

Thus, humans are not mere victims of environment. Their development is not a result of the mix of environment and heredity, with them the innocent bystanders, as it were. They can control the environment, their reactions to it, and direct their learning processes.

Christian teachers should always keep this intelligent purpose in mind as they seek to guide the learning process. Development toward the "perfect person" is the reason the ministry of teaching was given (Ephesians 4:13). Thus, the Christian teacher thinks in terms of biblical truth and spiritual influence and seeks to encourage a whole-person response to them.

Even the most experienced teachers are constantly learning about learning. It is safe to say that the last word on the subject has not been said yet. Nevertheless, many basic principles and laws have been observed in operation, and teachers will do well to incorporate them into their approaches. A clear understanding of them will lay a foundation for future success.

Key principles of learning are (1) the principle of interest, curiosity, and attention; (2) the principle of readiness; (3) the principle of exercise; (4) the principle of satisfying; and (5) the principles of retention. A brief look at each will be helpful at this point:

1. *The principle of interest, curiosity, and attention*—The root of the principle is interest, which is the identification of the learner with a person, activity, object, or idea. Interests may be either native or acquired. Curiosity is the hunger to know, the "mother" of learning. Usually it follows the lines of interest. Attention is focusing the mind's powers on the object or ideas of interest and may be voluntary (with effort) or involuntary (without effort). The teachers must see the students' interests and *create* interests.

2. *The principle of readiness*—Sometimes called mind-set, this principle means just what the term denotes, a readiness to learn or act. A readiness to learn can be both maturational (mental age) and psychological. It touches on ability and desire. In the case of reading readiness, for example, it usually means ability, while psychological readiness can be compared to mood. A readiness to learn makes the difference between forcing students to learn and enticing or leading them.

3. *The principle of exercise*—Sometimes called the principle of repetition, or use and disuse, it is universally recognized as an integral part of the learning process. Learning results from physical, mental, or emotional self-activity and exercise. The student learns by doing. "Let me try!" is often the plea of small children trying a new venture. They have already discovered they learn how to do something by doing it.

4. *The principle of satisfying*—Some have called this the fundamental principle of learning. In simple terms, it states that learning accompanied by satisfaction occurs more readily, while learning accompanied by dissatisfaction,

annoyance, or unpleasantness tends to be resisted or even rejected. If the students find answers and derive pleasure from learning, they will want to continue. The students will tend to derive pleasure if the learning is relative to their interests and desires.

5. *The principles of retention*—Memory is essential to learning. The ability to retain and recall is the basis of advanced learning. Therefore, any principle that will facilitate this ability should be utilized by the teacher. The following four laws should be observed:

   a. The law of impression—Vivid impression aids memory. Attention, imagination, and concentration are active when the impression is vivid. Stories that live, illustrations that paint pictures in the mind, and startling facts or questions create vivid impressions.

   b. The law of association—Students tend to remember more readily if what they learn can be associated in some way with what they already know. The use of comparison and contrast is the chief technique here.

   c. The law of meaningfulness—Meaningful material is retained much more readily than meaningless material. Clear understanding is the secret here. Using questions, restatement, illustrations, and examples can greatly aid in making the concepts clear.

   d. The law of repetition—Repetition tends to aid memory. Repetition must be meaningful and must be done actively not passively, with attention and not mechanically. Repetition includes review, which often involves restatement. It may also include summary and overview, as well as bringing in relationships between parts and wholes. Thus, meaningfulness and repetition as principles work together.

Motivation

Motivation occupies a significant place in the whole learning process. Analyzing its nature and identifying means by which the teacher can motivate learning will be helpful.

A motive is an inner state that incites action, energizes, or moves, and directs or channels human behavior toward goals. It may be any need, desire, wish, drive, idea, emotion, or state that prompts action. It is spoken of sometimes as a "striving condition," directed toward a given goal, object, condition, or activity.

Motivation is the cause of learning. It is what activates, sustains, and directs learning; it is the *why* of learning. Adequate and proper motivation must be present if learning is to be effective. Any who have taught have faced the question, "Why study this?" For this reason, the what and how of knowledge or skill cannot be carried very far in the learning situation until the why has been cared for.

Various attempts have been made to group motives, but none of them is totally adequate. There are physiological motives, stemming from the physical needs. There are psychological motives, stemming from a wide selection of needs, many of them learned. There are spiritual motives, stemming from people's spiritual nature. The motivation to worship and to have divine approval would be in that grouping.

An approach teachers may find useful is to distinguish between *intrinsic* and *extrinsic* motives:

1. *Intrinsic motivation rests in the subject matter to be learned and its relation to the learner in the satisfaction of "felt needs."* When the student is interested in the activity or the material to be learned, when satisfaction results from learning certain material for its own sake, then the motivation is said to be intrinsic. The material's inherent worth or value and its association with the learners'

ideals and life-goals are the source of the motivation. Obviously the learners' previously adopted value systems will affect what will have intrinsic motivation for them.

Intrinsic motivation has a long-range and durable effect. Often, however, it does not seem adequate for the immediate situation, although the point is debatable.

2. *Extrinsic motivation is external to the learning process itself, but is not necessarily artificial.* The motivation rests with the learners, their wants, drives, and desires. Praise, blame, prizes, honor, "stars," and many forms of commendation, approval, or recognition are extrinsic motivation.

Teachers must evaluate extrinsic motives on the basis of not only how they affect learning, but also what attitudes, emotions, and possible conflicts they may evoke. Competition is an example in point. Often contests and prizes can result in conflict. They need not, however, if adequate rules and safeguards are set up and essential goals are kept in view.

It is interesting to note that Jesus sought to provide motivation for His students. He sought to release not just temporary, but lasting motives:

1. *Jesus based His motivation on a revelation of divine truth, very much an intrinsic motive.* In His view, what could have greater worth? Thus, He revealed truth, truth as it was in Him. He revealed God and the way to God. Then He showed why one should love God and serve Him.

2. *He appealed to other intrinsic motives.* For example, He said, " 'If you love me, you will obey what I command' " (John 14:15).

3. *He appealed to certain extrinsic motives.* He promised reward. " 'These things will be given to you as well' " (Matthew 6:33). Again, He said, " 'I am coming soon! My reward is with me' " (Revelation 22:12).

4. *He appealed to conscience as a motive.* " 'You *should* have practiced the latter, without neglecting the former' " (Matthew 23:23; italics added). And again, "they *should* always pray" (Luke 18:1; italics added).

5. *He taught that the Holy Spirit would provide motivation.* " 'You will receive *power* when the Holy Spirit comes on you; and you will *be* my witnesses' " (Acts 1:8; italics added).

While many lists of motives or needs have been compiled and none of them is exhaustive, the following list may be helpful: the need to acquire, to preserve oneself, to express oneself, to enhance oneself or one's position, to order things (to organize, to be tidy and clean), to retain, to build, to achieve, to receive recognition, to be wanted, to be loved, to love, to dominate, to be autonomous, to be different, to avoid blame, to be helpful, to relax and have fun, to explore.

The teachers' task is to motivate students to learn. In doing so, they should appeal to both intrinsic and extrinsic motives, touching on a wide variety of needs that tend to move the students.

Gradually, however, Christian educators will seek to move toward intrinsic motivation. They will guide the students in establishing ideals, higher goals, and uplifting motives. Some of the their most effective work can be done in this area, not in the volume of content mastered but in the values espoused, the goals adopted, the incentives accepted, the ideals sought—all of which will continue to motivate and guide the ensuing learning process even when the teachers are no longer present. In short, turning on the "light in the eye" which draws toward continued learning is the ultimate goal.

Motivating Learning

Various methods have been employed in an effort to motivate learning. Students respond in different ways and to different appeals. As much as possible, teaching should allow for differences. However, the general approaches suggested here apply to most students. A teacher can provide motivation through the following:

1. *A guided learning experience*—Usually the experience, should be pleasant, enjoyable, and rewarding. However, occasionally it may be unpleasant, offering only the reward of learning. Even difficulties and frustrations can have their learning value. Each class session should be a planned learning experience with personal involvement included. Jesus used that type of approach. He taught His disciples; He showed them, ministering as they looked on; then He sent them out to "try." Afterward He evaluated their experiences with them.

2. *Goal setting*—Setting goals for achievement provides motivation. In memory work it is used in an elementary way. Goal setting is obvious in the whole structure of higher education—series of courses, levels of work, degrees, etc. A teacher who helps students "see" what they can do with their lives and how they can achieve their goals does a great thing. Through suggestions and encouragement, the teacher can help the students set immediate and long-range goals that will become the great motivations of their lives.

Jesus set goals for Nathanael, Peter, and Andrew when He called them. To Nathanael He said, " 'You shall see heaven open, and the angels' " (John 1:51). To Peter and Andrew He said, " 'I will make you fishers of men' " (Matthew 4:19). Later to Peter He said, " 'Blessed are you . . . You are Peter . . . I will give you the keys' " (Matthew 16:17–19). Jesus motivated them to think about what they might do and become.

3. *An example in the excitement of learning*—Teachers who enjoy learning, who are always discovering something new and sharing it, will have students who want to do the same.

45

Teachers who are deeply involved in their subjects will involve their students as well. It is reported that Dr. Wilbur Smith, a well-known Bible teacher, often opened class with these words, "I found something new this morning!"

4. *Using rewards of various kinds*—Both intrinsic and extrinsic rewards, satisfactions, and accomplishments are effective. Nothing can replace a smile of approval, a word of commendation, or a combination of constructive criticism and subsequent commendation.

5. *Using assignments and tests*—In the Christian education setting, the assignments and tests may be brief. They may even be simply the use of questions and answers during the class session, but the motivational value of fixing a responsibility to learn and holding the learner accountable is nonetheless there.

6. *Relating the lessons and learning to life needs*—The many needs, drives, desires, and interests previously noted are bridges into the students' minds, the starting point of learning. If what is to be learned is of personal value and meaning, and relative to the students' lives, they will tend to want to learn.

7. *Seizing on the various divine appeals*—Learning and serving God out of duty; out of love for God, for His Work, for His Word, for His people; for the rewards and fulfillment He offers—these motivations appeal to the highest in human nature and have spurred songwriters, great preachers, missionaries, and even martyrs!

8. *Appealing to a scriptural command*—"Study to show thyself approved" (2 Timothy 2:15, KJV). Such an appeal is unique to Christian education.

9. *Leading to an experience with Christ, to the baptism in the Holy Spirit*—To receive Christ and to be filled with the Spirit are the most deeply motivating experiences a person can know. A desire

to learn God's Word and to know God better are intrinsic to those experiences. The Holy Spirit is sent to lead to truth and to teach.

10. *The personal "weight" of the teacher*—One key to motivating learning is found in the position of teacher itself. As a guide to learning, as counselors and friends, teachers occupy a place of example held by few in the students' lives. If the teachers are respected and appreciated, what they say can go a long way in helping each of their students as they adopt goals, accept values, exert effort, and in many other ways set before themselves the path of learning they will follow. The teachers' Christian experiences and the wholeness of their growing Christian lives are the factors to which they must give attention if they would, in turn, motivate others.

❋ ❋ ❋ ❋

4

Teaching That Leads To Change

Broadly defined, teaching is causing the student to learn. It is often thought of in terms of imparting information, or imparting knowledge or skill. Hence, those who have attempted to teach have devoted their talents and energies to covering the lesson. They have concerned themselves with getting through the lesson rather than getting the lesson through. The basic approach has been "you sit here and be quiet while I teach you the lesson." It has generally been assumed that covering the lesson in the time allotted equals good teaching. Little or no concern has been given to the involvement of students.

Testimony to the fallacy of this approach is easily seen in the generation that can retell Bible stories, orally relate the Church's traditions and doctrines, and talk about Christian principles with all the proper vocabulary and yet demonstrate, in life, a hollow void. Their lives and their knowledge tell different tales. Truth is not personified in their lives.

One cannot help but ask, *If these students do not live like Christians, have they really learned what it is to be a Christian?*

Experience and action seem closely related to teaching and learning. If we ask if the students have truly learned, we must also ask if those who have taught them have truly taught. When teachers go through the motions of preparing and presenting lessons, but no change is shown in the students, one rightly may ask if the teachers have really taught.

Etymologically speaking, the word *teach* is derived from the Anglo-Saxon word *taecean*, which basically means "to show how to do." Note that the word is a transitive verb which needs an object. The subject does something to the object (e.g., "The boy threw the ball"). Teaching means doing something to the learner.

Teaching implies learning. *The teacher has not taught until the student has learned.* Therefore, it is quite possible for the teacher to go through the motions of selecting subject matter, performing a series of operations (including assigning, explaining, requiring various forms of practice and testing), with the purpose of transmitting the subject matter to the student without really teaching anything. Change must happen to the student. Learning must take place before the teacher has taught. Just as the salesman has not sold until the customer has bought, the teacher has not taught until the student has learned.

For too long, Sunday School teachers have proceeded on the erroneous assumption that knowledge of Bible content will result in Christian character and relationship. Experience has proven the error of this assumption. Christian teachers must, while holding that the Bible is basic and fundamental, lead the students through the process of encountering the Bible content, assimilating it into their own lives, then proceeding to make choices and perform actions that are thoroughly Christian.

Our teaching task is not complete until the students demonstrate in daily living all the truths that are contained in the

Bible. Bible knowledge is not an end in itself, but rather, a means to an end.

Learning

The learning process, then, is more than sitting quietly, listening, and memorizing. It is the active process of encountering, assimilating, and acting on the information. Likewise, teaching is guiding the students in the active process so that they will encounter, assimilate, and act on the information. Both teaching and learning are vitally linked in an active process. Hence, we talk in terms of the teaching-learning process.

Learning is an experience. We learn by doing. Learning best takes place when there is interaction between the teacher, the student, and the information. There must be personal involvement with the material intellectually, emotionally, or physically, by either formal or informal means. Learning is greatly increased when involvement with the material occurs on all the levels. Therefore, the teacher's choice of methodology greatly affects the teaching-learning process. The wise teacher varies the methodology in any class session to cause involvement on all of the levels.

Behaviorists define learning as change in behavior. There is, without doubt, much truth in that observation. Implied, however, in the definition is the idea that each succeeding generation builds on the experience of previous generations and adds to that the discoveries of its own. That would mean each generation is improved over the previous one. If pursued long enough, this should eventually lead to utopia. Humans should gain sufficient knowledge to cure all their ills. Thus, education is the hope of the world.

This point of view fails to take into account the basic human nature. People are not improving. Humans have, in reality, not progressed far from Cain and Abel. Their basic problem is that they are morally and spiritually degenerate and powerless to help themselves. Casual observation of society will reveal the effects of this condition. The evidence is all about us. With all people's attempts to improve themselves, they still fall short of what they must be.

Only regeneration can solve people's basic problem. Education will not, therefore, produce a panacea. Christian education, however, provides the opportunity for change to occur. It is only as a degenerate person comes into a right relationship to God through Jesus Christ that problems are solved. Herein lies the hope of the world.

Change

While educational change is difficult to define and even more difficult to measure, modification and adjustment should be expected in a variety of individual characteristics, such as knowledge, skills, interests, attitudes, values, beliefs, personality traits, relationships, and behavior. As these attributes increase, the individual tends to become less dogmatic, authoritarian, and prejudicial. There is generally a trend toward increasing intellectual interests and capacities as well as the tendency to value aesthetics more highly. Personality development tends toward greater independence, self-confidence, and the ability and willingness to express one's impulses and ideas. Thus, educational change is generally thought of as increasing maturity or growth.

Change is a vital part of learning. Neither teaching nor learning has happened until the student is changed. Change, however, must begin on a proper basis, which is spiritual in nature. All educational change is basically summarized in three areas—change in knowledge, change in attitude, and change in conduct—but all are predicated on a changed relationship to God.

Bedrock to the Christian message is the promise of a changed life. Christian converts have a new relationship to God. They are no longer alienated and estranged from God. Instead, they have been adopted into God's family and become His children. Water baptism is a fitting symbol of the converts' changed lives. They are raised to walk in newness of life. Their attitudes and desires are changed. They cease to find pleasure in living to please self and find their highest pleasure in living to glorify God.

Christian education derives its mission and message from the Bible. The Master Teacher laid down teaching objectives for Christian teachers. Christ's Great Commission to His disciples was to teach. As reported by Matthew, the Great Commission carries the idea of initial teaching that leads to Christian conversion, continued discipline that results in church membership, and continual teaching that leads to Christian living.

The church's mission necessitates that the teaching ministry be resident in the church. Ephesians 4:12–14 suggests that the church's mission is to help mature the saints. Spiritual maturity is the goal of Christian teaching. We are also told in this passage that spiritual maturity is "measuring to the stature of the fullness of Christ." Reproduction of Christlikeness in the believers' lives is the task of Christian teaching. This, as well as the Great Commission, suggests that our task is first to win people to Jesus Christ, then to help them grow in Him.

Growth is a major part of learning. As the student encounters, assimilates, and acts on the Bible lesson, growth and maturity in Christlikeness result. Spiritual growth is a process that is never completed. It begins with spiritual birth, continues throughout life, and is never fully attained. We are continually becoming like Christ, yet without ever becoming fully like Him. But we shall be like Him. First John 3:2 tells us that when He shall appear, we shall be like Him; for we shall see Him as He is. The church's mission is to bring people to Christ and to train them in Christ. The church is to evangelize and to educate. We must both reach people and teach people.

Since our task is to help persons become Christlike by receiving Jesus Christ as Lord and Savior and growing to spiritual maturity, we must conduct each class session in such fashion as to achieve these objectives. Thus, we reaffirm that Christian teaching is person-centered rather than program-centered. Each lesson must focus on the students' needs. We do not teach in a vacuum. Our lessons must be related to life. Each lesson must contain that which can be applied in life after leaving the classroom.

Christian teaching assumes that the Bible is the all-sufficient rule for faith and practice. Hence each lesson must be so designed as to lead the student through the steps of encountering, assimilating, and acting on God's Word with a life-relatedness that is as up-to-date as the day after tomorrow. Not until believers are able to apply the truth to their lives have we really taught, or have they really learned.

How To Teach To Lead To Change

Teachers must, therefore, concern themselves with the question of how to bring about teaching-learning that leads to changed lives. Several things must be borne in mind if the process is to be accomplished. Teachers must be familiar with the various steps in the teaching-learning process. Ligon articulates five steps in the process that every teacher should observe:[1]

1. *The first step is exposure.* It is only the beginning. It is an introduction to the idea, an encounter with the information.

2. *The second step is repetition.* Educators have long known the value of repeating the idea. The wise teacher will vary the classroom experience to communicate the same single idea from many perspectives. The room arrangement, the bulletin board,

the songs that are chosen, the approach to the lesson content, the expressional activity should all repeat the same basic idea from different perspectives.

3. *The third step is understanding.* If the students are to assimilate the lesson content and personalize it, they must understand it. The students must know the meaning of the words and be familiar with the ideas, demands, and concepts being presented.

4. *The fourth step is conviction.* Encountering the ideas and thoroughly understanding them is not enough. The learners must come to the point of certainty about the ideas. They must develop strong convictions and implement those convictions in their own lives.

5. *The fifth step is application.* The Scriptures repeatedly teach that we are to be doers as well as hearers of the Word. James says, "Faith divorced from deeds is lifeless as a corpse" (James 2:26, New English Bible). Learning is not only encountering and assimilating, but also acting on the information. Lois LeBar points out that a "student's growth is determined not only what he hears, but by what he does about what he hears."[2]

In guiding the learning experience, the teacher should provide classroom opportunities for the student to do the idea being conveyed or to discover ways to transfer it into action after leaving the classroom.

The teacher who applies these five steps to the teaching-learning situation will contribute greatly in assuring that learning will take place.

Teachers also should be aware of teacher-student relationships. Bigge and Hunt state, "We may imagine three broad types of relationships between teacher and students: (1) authoritarian, (2) laissez-faire, and (3) democratic."[3] They contend that each of these types of relationships produces a distinctive situation within the classroom that is characterized by more or less predictable results.

In the authoritarian situation, teachers are central. They exercise firm control and direct every action of the students. The teachers plan the classes, give all the directions, and practically tell the students what to think and how to act, without regard for the students' feelings. The students are the passive recipients of the information. Bigge and Hunt suggest that the authoritarian situation leads to apathy, noninvolvement, and resentment.

On the opposite end of the spectrum is the laissez-faire situation. Here the students are central. The teachers do not really lead at all. They are the passive element of the teaching-learning process. The students decide what they want to do and how they will do it. Bigge and Hunt show that, while this situation has some desirable improvements over the authoritarian situation, the students tend to be insecure. They are never quite sure what they should do or if they are doing it right.

Midpoint between these two is the democratic situation. Here both the teacher and the learner are active participants in the teaching-learning process. Neither is passive. There is a mutual give-and-take. Interchange between the students and from the students to the teacher is welcomed. Bigge and Hunt, again, show that this situation results in a higher level of efficiency. Generally, it utilizes the strengths of both of the other situations and minimizes their limitations. Thus the teacher should guide the students in the process of encountering, assimilating, and acting on the material by encouraging their involvement in the teaching-learning process.

Teaching that leads to change means the teacher should be aware of certain principles of teaching-learning. Many lists of such principles have been written. The following list is not intended to be exhaustive, only representative:

1. *Teachers must begin where the students are.* This means the

teachers must know the students. They should be acquainted with the age-level characteristics and developmental tasks of their groups. Teachers should also know every individual student well enough to know how that student conforms to and differs from the average for the student's age-level. Such knowledge can come only by involvement with the students on an individual basis.

2. *The teachers must move from the known to the unknown.* Teachers cannot expect students to follow them when the students do not know where the teachers are going. This concept is as ancient as time. Isaiah wrote, "Precept must be upon precept, precept upon precept; line upon line, line upon line; here a little and there a little" (Isaiah 28:10).

This again emphasizes the need of knowing what a student at a particular level is able to comprehend, as well as knowing what that individual child can comprehend. Much of what is taught in the church is abstract truth. Children are not used to thinking in terms of abstractions. They are far more used to thinking of blocks and trucks and dolls than in terms of kindness, love, and character. To help them grow in Christian precepts, the teacher must lead them along a path from where they are to where they are headed. To do this the teacher must move slowly from the known to the unknown.

3. *The teacher should make the basic assumption that each student can improve.* Students learn at different rates. Some are challenged to learn more by one means than another. Some are easier to lead along the path of discovery, but every student can grow and learn. Interest is vitally tied up with change. The elements of the class period should, therefore, appeal to the students' interests. The teacher can greatly enhance the chances of learning and change by seriously appealing to the students on the basis of their interests.

4. *Teaching must be in terms of the students' needs.* Students are not apt to learn and will be changed little or none at all unless the lesson meets their particular needs. The teachers should see that each lesson contains that which will meet the needs of those in the class. Unless the students can relate the truths to the experiences of life there can be no transfer, or carryover, from lesson to life. This is of utmost importance if teaching-learning is to happen. The truths taught must fit life. Therefore, the illustrations, visuals, expressional activities, etc., must be life-related.

5. *Students learn from the teachers' actions as well as from their speech.* The teachers who cannot apply Christian principles in their own lives cannot expect any application in the students' lives. Change and motivation to change happens on a nonverbal basis as the students observe their teachers' lives.

The Teacher's Responsibilities to the Church

Teachers must see their responsibilities in terms of the total ministry of the church. No single ministry of the church can contribute to a life all that is needed to assist a person in becoming a whole being. The church's program grows out of the needs of the people who make up the church and should be designed to minister to those needs.

Luke 2:52 gives the only record of Jesus's life from the time He was twelve years old until He began His public ministry at the age of thirty. This lone verse simply says that He grew physically, intellectually, spiritually, and socially. Those four areas represent the areas of basic human need. There must be proper growth in all of the areas if the individual is to be a whole, balanced person.

While no single experience can meet the needs of all four areas, teachers should become aware of what part their ministries contribute in the mission of building whole persons to the honor of God. Although the teachers, in one class period a week, cannot meet all the needs, they must vitally concern themselves that all the needs are cared for.

The teachers must recognize their roles in the total ministry of the church. They must be just as faithful and loyal to all aspects of the life, witness, and fellowship of the church as they are to their own areas of ministry. This faithfulness should be demonstrated by active participation in the church's services and ministries. Teachers would do well to strive to get all their students to attend such meetings. After the students are there, the teachers should observe them and avail themselves of any opportunity to pray, counsel, or share with the students. Their total spiritual development should be the teachers' concern.

The Teacher's Responsibilities to Teaching

The teacher teaches out of the abundance of a full life. The teacher whose life is shallow cannot expect to teach in such a fashion as to build full lives. Teaching is being, not just doing or telling. Teachers should, therefore, seek throughout the week to build themselves into whole, balanced Christians.

A prime requisite for a good teacher is a vital, dynamic, growing relationship with Jesus Christ. Such growth is never complete. We are ever becoming more like Jesus, but in this life we will never become fully like Him. As we are constantly growing into His image, we have a fuller life and background from which to draw for the teaching situation. The teacher, therefore, must develop personal Bible study and prayer habits. We come to know more of Christ and become more like Him as we encounter Him in the written Word and as we pray.

For personal enrichment, the teacher should pursue several areas of study. These studies are in addition to lesson preparation, which will be our concern in a later study. The teacher should engage in the lifelong task of mastering the Bible. Survey studies, book studies, topical studies, biographical studies, doctrinal studies would all fit into personal-enrichment studies. The teacher should also strive to become a better teacher by continued study. This course is only an introductory study. There will be need for further study in educational principles and psychology. The teacher should continue to study the characteristics and needs of students, new and improved methods of teaching, audiovisuals, etc.

To help accomplish this personal enrichment, the teacher will want to begin building a personal library, as well as taking advantage of the church library and community services, such as public or college libraries. The teacher should subscribe to several good, high-quality evangelical, Christian education periodicals.

The teacher should also take advantage of opportunities for more training through seminars, conferences, conventions, and further training classes. The annual workers training study and monthly workers conference should be considered a must by the teacher.

Early in the week, while Sunday's class time is still clearly in mind, the teacher should evaluate the session, and ask these questions: *Was a particular item a success or failure? Why? What could have improved it? Were the lesson objectives met?* No lesson is ever so perfect that improvements could not have been made. Honest evaluation is a wholesome process and can lead to improved teaching.

The Teacher's Responsibilities to the Students

Dr. Howard Hendricks, professor of Christian education at Dallas Theological Seminary, tells that his mother was religious while his father was atheistic. His parents separated before his birth and he never saw them together except in the divorce court in Philadelphia when he was eighteen years old.

Howard's family was unconcerned about his spiritual welfare. In his community in Philadelphia a group of people started a church. Walt, a tall man from the church, found Howard playing marbles. After a negative response to his invitation to attend his Sunday School class, Walt asked Howard if he would like to learn to play marbles. After several games, Walt began to show the boy how to hold a marble to get a more accurate and powerful shot. The love this man demonstrated penetrated Howard so that he would have followed Walt anywhere. The next Sunday, Howard joined twelve other boys, who had been brought in by similar means, in Walt's class.

The interesting facts are that eleven of those thirteen boys are in fulltime Christian work; nine of them came from broken homes; and Walt never went beyond the sixth grade. The success of Walt's ministry was found in the fact that he loved these boys for Christ's sake. Walt continued to build this relationship by teaching the boys on Sunday and going places with them during the week.

This teacher caught the vision that his responsibility was more than just a Sunday job. He recognized that the largest part of his ministry was conducted during the week.

The teacher's contact with the students throughout the week should be seen as an opportunity to teach by example. Time spent with class members during the week provides the opportunity to demonstrate in life the concepts taught in the class. Through-the-week contacts with the students show the teacher's interest in them, and such contacts also constitute a laboratory in life. The wise teacher will, therefore, seek to make opportunities to be with the students during the week. The perceptive teacher will thereby discover the students' needs and interests.

Teachers should use their contacts with the students during the week as an opportunity for ministry. Many of the students will be in need of personal, individualized spiritual help. Some may make this fact known in the class; others may attempt to hide their needs. Teachers should always be perceptive of these needs and use the weekday contacts to minister to them. In some cases students may feel more inclined to share their needs with a teacher than with the pastor. Ministry throughout the week may well include counseling, prayer for the sick, and so forth.

Visitation of students during the week provides an opportunity for ministry. Guests should be visited in their homes during the week immediately following their visit to class. The interest and concern shown in this gesture may be the invitation that is needed for the student to return and become a regular member of the class. There is always a reason why persons visit a church. Many times the reason is a recognition of needs that can be met only by spiritual means. The teacher who fails in this responsibility has failed indeed.

Contact with absentees should also be viewed as an opportunity for spiritual ministry. There are obviously many reasons why students are absent from class. Undoubtedly every student sometimes misses class. The reasons for these absences may be rooted in deep spiritual need, sickness, or less crucial problems like being out of town or simply oversleeping. Some churches require teachers to make personal contact with all absentees during the week following the absence.

There are many appropriate means of contact that will fit the need. Written contact, either by letter, e-mail, or postcard, may be appropriate. In some cases a phone call may be adequate.

Certainly the personal visit is usually in order. Habitual absence should usually be followed by a personal visit from the teacher.

Periodically the teacher should make a home visit to every class member. The students should not come to think that the only way their teacher will come see them is for them to be absent. The faithful student also deserves the interest of a personal call or e-mail. Even the student who is regular in attendance may need personal ministry that can be given only during the week. It would be wise for the teacher to telephone in advance of going to a home, particularly where the family is not known well.

The teacher should periodically plan social experiences. These are also opportunities for spiritual ministry. Since one area of human need is social, the teacher will help mature the students with an appropriate, well-planned class social time. These experiences can help build a more lasting friendship between the teacher and the students as well as among the students. They may serve as evangelistic opportunities, times of fellowship, Bible study, and devotion.

The teacher's through-the-week ministry should also include time for personal evangelism. Winning converts to Jesus Christ and teaching them in the way of Jesus Christ are parallel tasks. The Great Commission requires both. The teacher should develop skills of communicating the gospel to the unconverted. This ministry may take the form of prospect hunting for the class—as Walt's ministry did—but should come within the teacher's responsibility as a Christian.

Some teachers will want to structure evangelism ministries for the class to participate in. A class project or a service at a mission, nursing home, hospital, or children's home, would be most fitting to help the students come to live and share what is being taught in the classroom.

Throughout the week the teacher should seek to build

wholesome, mutually beneficial relationships with other teachers. These should be opportunities for spiritual and personal enrichment. Teachers may find solutions to classroom problems as they discuss and pray about those problems with peers. Successes may prove to be a real blessing to other teachers as they are shared in these encounters.

The teacher's responsibility does not end when the bell rings on Sunday morning. Teaching students is a full-time job. No area can be allowed to go without care. The person who responds to the calling to be a teacher accepts much responsibility. They must be true to that calling and minister throughout the week.

Endnotes

1. Earnest M. Ligon, *A Greater Generation* (New York: The Macmillan Company, 1948), 10–13.

2. Lois E. LeBar, *Education That Is Christian* (Westwood, N. J.: Fleming H. Revell Company, 1958), 136.

3. Morris L. Bigge and Maurice P. Hunt, *Psychological Foundations of Education* (New York: Harper & Row, 1962), 12.

✳ 5 ✳

Basic Teaching Methods

Lecture

Ask people to picture an adult Sunday School class, and most will picture a teacher lecturing to a room full of students. Lecture has long been the most common and popular method of teaching. There is much about lecturing to recommend itself when used properly. However, when used improperly, like any method, the lecture can prove detrimental to learning.

The advantages of using the lecture method are many:

1. *The lecture can be easily used with any size group and with any room arrangement.*

2. *It is the most time-efficient way to communicate large quantities of information.*

3. *It is usually more organized and stays on track better than most other methods.*

4. *It requires a minimum of mastery by teachers since they only present what they know and keep personal control of where the lesson will go.*

5. *The teachers' personalities and abilities greatly affect the lecture.* (This can also be a liability, depending on the lecturer.)

There are weaknesses to counterbalance some of the advantages of lecturing:

1. *Lecturing often fails to accommodate student involvement; therefore, personalization and application tend to be low.*

2. *Teachers who lecture often find it difficult to break the pattern, so they rely on lecturing almost exclusively.*

3. *Lecturing encourages passivity and stifles students' creativity.*

4. *It can condition students to believe anything the teacher says and fail to equip them to evaluate or work through issues on their own.*

5. *It provides little student feedback, so the teacher is unable to adjust and tailor the lesson to meet students' needs.*

The basic method of lecturing is a good one and should be a part of every teacher's repertoire. However, always remember that lecturing, like any other method, should never be the only method employed in a lesson. Variety is the key. Different students learn in different ways. It is important to use different teaching approaches to meet the needs of all students. But don't choose your methodology solely on the basis of variety. Balance several factors to determine what to use, including which methods you are most comfortable with, the interests of your students, and the points to be made. Some points lend themselves particularly well to one type of methodology over another.

Here are some important points to remember when using the lecture method:

1. *Prepare well.* Organize your lesson carefully. You may consider duplicating an outline to give to the students so they can follow along as you go.

2. *Don't try to present too much.* Develop a clear, concise outline with logical progression and a manageable amount of material to cover.

3. *Speak clearly.* Speak loudly enough to be heard, but in a natural, pleasing tone. Vary your pace and volume. Use inflection and pitch effectively. Maintain eye contact with the students.

4. *Develop clear objectives for the lesson and let the students know where the lecture is headed.*

5. *Never, never use lecture exclusively.* Always combine the lecture method with some other methodology that allows for student feedback and participation (discussion, buzz groups, case studies, circle response, etc.). Break up the lecture with visuals (chalkboard, overhead transparencies, posters, object lessons, demonstrations, etc.). Use interesting illustrations or anecdotes to create memorable word pictures.

6. *Emphasize important points.*

7. *Review what has been covered to reinforce learning.*

Variations that can spice up a lecture include choral reading, flipcharts, guest lecturers, interviews, recorded stories, and symposiums. (Note: a choral reading is a Scripture passage arranged to be read dramatically by students in a series of group readings, solos, and ensembles. A symposium is a series of speeches given by as many speakers as there are aspects of an issue.)

When preparing the classroom for a successful lecture, make every effort to minimize distractions. Undue noise, an unpleasant environment, or open windows to gaze through detract from learning, compete with the teacher for the students' attention, and should be reduced or eliminated.

Finally, lecturers should seek to inspire their classes to see the large picture rather than just bits of information. They should open up problems and issues and consider possible solutions and answers. Their desire should be to motivate students to think, then to let them fill in the details and implications for themselves.

Storytelling

Storytelling, one of the most ancient methods of teaching, develops character in young and old alike by changing attitudes. The storytelling method imparts knowledge, captures and holds interest, arouses and stimulates imagination, and most often leads to strong emotional appeal. While combining characterization and plot setting, storytelling presents truth in action, makes the needed connection between the known and the unknown, presents abstract truth in concrete terms, incites readiness to learn, and makes its own positive application.

To prevent the student from becoming passively involved in the teaching-learning experience and to prevent the story from becoming mere entertainment, the teacher should seriously consider how and when to use the storytelling method. Like most other methods, it should not be used as the only method of the class session. Storytelling may be advantageously used (1) to introduce the lesson by focusing attention on the central problem or theme of the lesson; (2) in the development of the learning experience by illustrating some difficult point; (3) in making application of the truth; or (4) as the conclusion to the class hour.

If the story is presented improperly, the students may merely learn the narrative and fail to associate any principle with it. Overuse of the storytelling method may result in the students' inability to gather facts, solve problems, and engage in other kinds of learning that involve independent thinking.

Choosing an appropriate story is a major part of good story-telling. Stories, sometimes used to hold interest, can also be used to explain or illustrate a point. Some stories provide a mental example, while others can be used to emphasize a point. Whatever the story's purpose, the teacher should be certain that its effect will be in direct proportion to the desire or need.

Another consideration in choosing the appropriate story is the audience. Knowledge of the age-level characteristics and of individual class members will greatly enhance the value of the story. Students' interests are in direct relationship to their abilities. Small children, who live in a world of make-believe or of "let's pretend," may be appealed to by fantasy. The older child tends to identify with the hero of the story, so stories for children of this age should lead them down a pathway of discovery and adventure. Young people respond readily to a story that portrays idealism or romance, while adults, concerned about the cares of life, find that stories based in realism are more helpful. Even a good story should not be used if it is inappropriate for the age-level being taught.

The teacher should also think clearly about the lesson aim. Since the story is part of the total teaching procedure and is often remembered long after the rest of the lesson is forgotten, the teacher should be certain the story clearly teaches the lesson that is to be learned and remembered.

Don't get caught up in your story and go on too long. Plan in advance how long the story should take and stick with that time frame. The story should be shaped to fit the rest of the lesson, rather than fitting the rest of the lesson to the story.

Before deciding on a story, carefully analyze the kinds of characters featured in central roles. Since students tend to put themselves into the leading role, the story should have the kind of hero with whom the students should identify. Some stories are so designed as to leave the hearer unconsciously siding with a villain. Without camouflaging the sins of people, the teacher would do well to avoid using stories that pit a villain against a hero. Because identification can be a powerful force for good, the teacher should think through all possible relationships the students may make.

All stories fit into either the true or the fictional category. If a story is true, care must be taken to see the details are accurate. If a story is fictional (that is, one that is made up) it should be clearly identified as such.

Stories may also be categorized as (1) open-ended, (2) complete, or (3) continued. The open-ended story is a device for stimulating discussion. Only that part of the story is told that is needed to set the stage for meaningful discussion of the problem. The class then, through discussion of the alternatives, builds the conclusion to the story.

The complete story, one in which the whole narrative is told, is used to explain an idea or give an example of it. The continued story is one in which only a part of it is told at each telling. This type of story is usually used to maintain continued interest. Each telling should end on a suspense-filled note that will invite the students to return time after time to avoid missing any part of the story.

The teacher, in telling a story, becomes an artist who paints a vivid and beautiful picture with words. To do this the story should be told with sincerity and naturalness. Storytellers should use their own words to describe the scene. It is essential to forget oneself and get into the story. Never should the audience feel the storyteller is talking down to them.

Unnecessary gestures only draw attention to the speaker, but as the story begins to flow, with emotion from the heart, the proper gestures will be used.

Whenever possible, storytellers should insert dialogue. A change in pitch or tone of voice to suit the characters will add interest. Wording of the dialogue should suit the character too. A king, shouldn't sound like a hobo and vice versa.

Vary the pace of the words for slow action, rapid action, a climax, rhythm. Use the pause in various ways—at the end of the story, just before the climax. Combine the pacing with the tone of voice: a very soft tone for heightened suspense; a quickened, animated tone for exciting, rapid action.

While the teacher and students should become emotionally involved in the story, care should be taken to avoid oversensationalization. As the events dramatically unfold, the story should build toward a conclusion that will be the main point to be made. The story should end quickly without moralizing; an appropriate story will make its own point. Sound effects, created by background music from either a piano or a CD, may be used to create a desirable setting for a story.

Storytelling, though an old method, can be very effective if these basic concerns are observed.

Assignments and Reports

Assigning students material to study and report back to the class has proved valuable to actively involve students in the learning process. Fearing the risk of over-requiring, some teachers may be reluctant to use this technique. However, the teacher should assume the students want to learn, and strive to discover ways to cultivate that desire and to create exciting study experiences that will foster opportunities for the students to study and share their discoveries with other class members. Such opportunities can help the students identify problems, stimulate the desire to discover truth, put students in contact with truth, and test their acquisition and use of that truth.

This teaching technique offers several advantages:

1. *It teaches through self-activity in the learning process.*

2. *It affords the teacher the opportunity to involve all the students in the learning task.*

3. *It allows the teacher to closely watch each student's development.*

4. *The teacher can test what is being learned.*

5. *It helps carry over the lesson truth into the student's everyday life.*

In using assignments and reports, the teacher should observe (1) the assignment, (2) the student's study, and (3) the feedback to the class. To make the assignment meaningful to the students the teacher must plan carefully, make the instructions clear, and allow adequate time for the students to study and to report back to the class.

In guiding the students' studies, the teacher should stimulate interest, guide research, answer questions, and provide resources. The feedback should follow the lesson plan and give the students time to express the significance of their findings. Never make an assignment without following up on it.

This teaching method offers several options:

1. *Book reviews*—A student, or a group of students, reads, summarizes, and interprets an author's thoughts for the purpose of gaining information. As they read the book, the students should ask: What is the author saying? How does that relate to the assignment? The students will probably want to outline the book's significant points. Class time should then be given for the students to conversationally relate to the class the information that they have gained and show how it relates to the assignment. Allow time for the students to ask questions of the reviewer. The teacher would do well to end the discussion by calling back into focus the book's major points as they relate to the lesson.

2. *Inductive Bible study*—To determine what a Bible passage says, what it means, and how that will affect the individual's

life, the student should read and reread the passage several times. Without the aid of commentaries and study helps, the student should simply observe what is being said and draw conclusions from the text. Questions such as the following can prove valuable in drawing conclusions about what the meaning is for the individual's life: Who is the author? What is he saying in this passage? Why is he saying it? When did he say it? Where is he saying it? To whom is he saying it? What does he mean by what he is saying?

This kind of study can be done in the classroom or, probably more profitably, used as an assigned study that the students do on their own between classes. The class period could then be used to discuss their findings and the implications of those finds.

3. *Listening teams*—In anticipation of a lecture or video presentation, the teacher divides the students into groups, or appoints a small representative group, to research particular aspects of a subject. The research is done in advance. As the lecture is heard, or the video presentation is viewed, these particular aspects are noted. The listening team then may either query the speaker or make an oral report to the class. This type of activity is valuable to secure information or new ideas through specific directed study.

4. *Memorization*—Memory, the faculty to reproduce that which one has learned, is a means of gathering and storing facts in precise wording for later recall. While results of this ancient method can be easily measured, it assures only knowledge of the words not the meanings. Research shows adults can memorize with at least the same ease as children. Motivation to memorize should be intrinsic (the desire to know God's Word) rather than extrinsic (to win a prize). Memorizing the Lord's Prayer, a psalm, Bible verses, or a hymn is not a painful experience that needs any reward other than the satisfaction of

accomplishment and spiritual gain. Memorization should be of materials that will be used and can be done at home or in class.

5. *Research reports*—A personal or group assignment is given to gather information on a particular issue or problem through research. The students study as many available resources as possible to gain information about the subject. At a later meeting, the researchers report their findings to the whole class so everyone is enriched by their study.

The teacher should select or lead the class in determining issues worthy of study; approve the topic; provide motivation for the students; help the class realize the importance of and need for study; suggest possible resources for the group to use; if possible, provide resources; and help the group, if asked, to interpret the findings. The group should present its findings to the class in a report time. Questions and answers or discussion may follow to help apply the findings to life.

6. *Testing*—The primary purpose of testing is to provide review and extend the students' learning experience. The secondary purpose is to give them an opportunity to demonstrate what they have learned. Testing should cause the students to recall what they have learned and let them apply it to a situation for a learning experience. As the students prepare for the test, they restudy what has been learned, associate it together as a whole, and apply it to life. In completing the test, they again recall the material.

True-false, multiple choice, completion, matching, or essay questions may be given, but should be so constructed as to cause the students to think. The answers should not be obvious, nor should they be veiled in ambiguous or trick choices. Only essay responses can begin to accurately measure students' mastery at the higher levels of learning (restatement, relation, and realization). Therefore, teachers should occasionally include essay questions to better judge the students' progress.

Question and Answer

The question is one of the most valuable tools of instruction known. We have already noticed how Jesus used it so effectively. In most schools a great proportion of classroom time centers on the question and answer method. The question stirs the student to think, to digest, to assimilate, and to express. It touches the springs of interest and curiosity and causes the student to see different aspects of the topic under consideration. The question arouses mental activity and thereby aids greatly in the learning process. It can be conceived of as a spoon stirring the mix of ideas in the mind.

The "spirit of inquiry" animates the use of classroom questions. In some respects, then, it has a "mother of learning" position. A sequence of purposes in the use of questions can be as follows:

1. *To encourage recall*—It discovers what the student knows and reviews past studies. It can be used to show relationships and "wholes," thereby helping understanding.

2. *To restate or translate ideas into a different form*—For example, "Can you express the ideas in your own words?"

3. *To interpret facts, generalizations, and ideas*—Using comparison or contrast questions accomplishes this purpose and increases clarity.

4. *To apply an idea or concept to everyday life*—It moves an idea from the textbook and the theoretical and puts it on the practical level.

5. *To analyze an idea, concept, or conclusion*—The logic employed is brought into focus, and the "parts" are identified and related one to another. The basis for valid conclusion is exposed.

6. *To synthesize, to bring together*—In problem solving, proposed solutions or agreed-on courses of action are often a synthesis of ideas.

7. *To evaluate*—The exercise of judgment and decision-making are involved in evaluating questions and answers that call for a weighing of ideas or possible actions against the criteria in use.

Still another purpose of questions is to lead to action—"Will you repent and accept Jesus Christ as your Savior? Will you yield your entire life to Him and accept Him as your Lord?" The moment of decision and action is the final moment in teaching. At that point the matter rests with the student. Asking the question is the last thing the teacher can do.

Various kinds of questions can be identified:

1. *The factual question brings the facts into view.*

2. *The rhetorical question does not require an oral response but is used for emphasis.*

3. *The problem-solving question raises a problem and possible solution for discussion; it is a most stimulating kind of question.*

4. *The personal or application question seeks to relate the idea directly to the student.*

Questions may also be classified in terms of the interrogatives used: who, what, where, when, why, and how. The last two, *why* and *how,* open up the most challenging questions.

Principles that will guide in the most effective use of questions in the classroom include the following:

1. *Questions should be clear.* They should be direct and to the point, free from ambiguous and obscure wording.

2. *Questions should be definite.* The question should have one answer not several possible ones. An example of a confusing

question is, "What did Jesus do after He was tempted in the wilderness?"

3. *Questions should be within the learner's grasp.*

4. *Questions should deal with essentials.*

5. *Questions should be asked in a logical order, progressing toward the desired learning.*

6. *Questions should pertain to and include the whole class.* Asking the question first and then calling on someone to answer tends to accomplish this.

7. *Questions should be a part of the conversational style, the give-and-take of the class.*

8. *Questions should stimulate thought.* "Yes" and "no" questions tend to have little value. "Why" and "how" questions are better because usually the student must think to respond to them.

Evaluating and using student responses is an important part of the art of questioning. Incomplete and partially correct answers should be used as a basis for further questions. Students should be encouraged as they respond. Credit should be given where possible, and a rephrased or additional question asked so as to get the full answer.

The students' responses to questions serve as a key to what they have learned or think. Responses are the bridges the students build into their thinking. A wise teacher will use those bridges.

❊ ❊ ❊ ❊

✳ 6 ✳
Small-Group Activities

That we are in Christ and He is in us and unity in the Church are concepts that are difficult to express fully in words. They can be experienced, however, in rich fellowship and association. It is God's will to work in the Church, the body of believers, to work with it and to work through it. God has chosen not only to relate to individuals through His Son, but also to relate to groups of individuals (Matthew 18:20).

Thus, the Church is one place in society where a true sense of community and brotherhood can prevail. Groups of believers associating together, learning together, and working together for the good of each member, for the good of the whole group, and for others outside of the group aptly describes one role of the Church.

Theodore Newcomb has defined a group as "two or more persons bound together by common norms and interlocking roles." Groups are more than the sum of their parts. The sense of "weness" and group spirit is strong in a group. People relating together in interaction bring into play forces that multiply the contributions of individuals and enhance the experience of all. Thus the association, learning, and work of each are enriched. But it is the enrichment of *learning* through group activity to which we give primary attention in this lesson.

Interaction in Groups

The number of interpersonal relationships increases as a group grows. However, when a group becomes too large, this is not true, because individuals cannot relate to all individuals in the group, For example, two persons can relate in a pattern of two interpersonal relationships. However, three persons can relate in six. As these diagrams show, the number of relationships increases with group growth (four equals twelve possible relationships, five equals twenty possible relationships, etc.). As Martha M. Leypoldt has observed, the total relationships possible are equal to the number of persons in the group times one less than the number of persons. Thus, ten persons total a possible ninety relationships (10 x 9).[1]

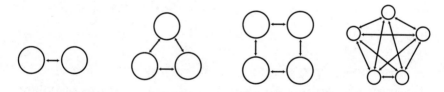

Whereas the possibility of greatly increased interpersonal relationships occurs mathematically in large groups, it actually decreases because of other limitations. Therefore, the size of the group is most important when one desires a single product from the group and individual enhancement and return. When the values of group interaction are sought, the group should be large enough to permit a number or variety of interpersonal relationships, and small enough to permit each member to relate to each other member in a meaningful way. A group of five to fifteen members usually permits this ideal, depending on the kind of group activity to be employed.

The physical setting and arrangement of a group can do much to encourage interaction. These diagrams show the possibilities in various settings.

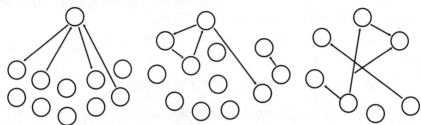

In the less formal and informal group settings, individuals face each other, relate to one another more readily, and feel free to participate. The resulting interaction is freer and more stimulating.

Members perform various roles as the group functions. To be effective, a group usually needs such formal roles as a discussion leader, a recorder, members-at-large, and sometimes an observer and/or a consultant. In many groups the teacher becomes the observer-consultant. In general, the five basic individual roles needed in a productive group are the following:

1. *Initiator*—one who sets forth an idea or initiates discussion.

2. *Enlarger*—one who seeks information that will enlarge the idea and shape it. This person imagines for the group and suggests other possibilities.

3. *Analyzer*—one who views the workability and implications of the idea or suggestion. This person is usually the logician of the group and sorts things out.

4. *Summarizer*—one who reviews and summarizes the developing idea, calling attention to what has been agreed on and what has been discarded.

5. *Organizer-implementer*—one who outlines what steps need to be taken to implement the idea or put it into action.

One individual may at times assume any one or all of these roles, as they are needed. In addition, many other mature supporting roles are involved in maintaining the group and in enabling it to pursue its work.

In applying the group method directly to teaching, various factors should be kept in mind:

1. *Each member's ideas and experiences have worth.*

2. *An atmosphere of mutual acceptance, trust, and confidence must prevail at all times.*

3. *People are more important than information. What happens to the person as a learner means more than covering a certain lesson or learning certain facts.*

4. *Goals are cooperatively adopted and worked at.*

Various ways of teaching in small groups are available to the imaginative teacher. They are adaptable to various age-levels in differing degrees. They include panels, symposiums, case studies, demonstrations, etc. Four more common group dynamic ways of teaching—discussion, projects, brainstorming, and buzz groups—will be enlarged on in this lesson.

Discussion

Few methods of teaching afford the range of possibilities the discussion method does. Few stimulate the class to involvement and participation as well. Often it has been said, "We had a good class today; we had a real good discussion!" The value of such teaching is self-evident.

A discussion consists of a group of individuals in an exchange of knowledge, ideas, and opinions, directed by a moderator, and aimed at a definite conclusion or decision. A discussion stems from a higher form of questioning in that it usually presents a more involved problem or group of problems and develops a line of thought. It involves group participation, but also individual mental activity. It results in sharing experiences, knowledge, and information, as well as formulating opinions and conclusions, and is a popular teaching method in both young people's and adult classes.

In a good discussion there should be mutual understanding and appreciation and each person should expect the other to contribute. Discussion is based on cooperative and group thinking and should result in a group decision. Occasionally agreement will not be achieved, but agreeableness should remain.

Among the goals sought in discussion are the following:

1. *To raise problems and attempt to discover solutions*

2. *To discover proper interpretations and applications of scriptural principles*

3. *To stimulate thinking and the desire to learn*

4. *To involve students who might otherwise not participate*

5. *To analyze through group thought, calling on the insights of various people*

Some teachers find it difficult to get a discussion going in their classes. Some conclude that their students do not like to discuss. To hear the students in the hall after class, however, will negate that conclusion. Often the problem centers in the teacher's failure to set up the conditions conducive to good discussion. Following are some essentials:

1. *A problem or question clearly set forth*—Usually the teacher will need to prime the pump, as it were, setting forth some of the issues on each side. Then the class will see the question's

significance and be eager to probe it.

2. *A purpose*—The discussion should fit into the lesson and contribute to it.

3. *A free exchange of ideas*—Knowledge, opinion, experience, and thought should be shared, with all contributing. Discussion, therefore, takes time.

4. *Open minds and tolerance of opinions*—Respect for others' opinions must be encouraged. The attitude should be, "Let's see what we can find out."

5. *Reflective thinking*—Discussion is not argument. It should be free from prejudice and preconceived ideas. Effort to bring all views into focus, to appeal to logic, to suggest rethinking or careful thinking will pay dividends.

6. *A qualified leader*—The leader must know how to stimulate and guide discussion and encourage others to participate.

7. *Adequate preparation by the members*—The ideal is for all to have studied and have something to contribute more than "off the top of their heads."

8. *A sincere desire to discover truth*—Other factors are important as well, such as the group's size and arrangement. The class should be small enough so all can share and be arranged informally so all can see each other. If a formal setting is employed where all look at the teacher but not at each other, the discussion will tend to be between the teacher and students, rather than among the students.

The discussion leaders (usually the teachers, but not necessarily) often determine the success of the discussion. Theirs is the task of encouraging discussion and filling in as needed. Six words can summarize their role: prepare, start, encourage, guide, summarize, and conclude.

Brainstorming

A brainstorming session is a group situation in which members attack a given problem, suggesting various possible solutions in a rapid-fire manner without evaluation. Neither negative nor positive comments about the suggestions are allowed until after the brainstorm itself is finished. Reasons why a solution will or will not work are reserved for the evaluation session that may follow.

Brainstorming requires a minimum of organization—just a leader and recorder and members-at-large. The group should have no more than twelve or fourteen members to allow for maximum participation by all and full tapping of potential resources. If the class is large, it is wise to separate it into subgroups of the suggested number, moving them to different areas of the room and suggesting they form circles. This will allow for maximum interaction.

The purpose of this type of group activity is to get fresh ideas, new solutions and approaches. Thus, it is widely used in industry, business, and science, and is applicable to the Christian education class as well.

Values of the brainstorming approach include the unrestricted thinking it incites, the elimination of negatives (often a member will have a good idea, but in other types of group activities will reject it before voicing it), and the opportunity for each member to participate. Shy members are drawn in to share; interest and spontaneous response are usually high; and all enjoy a pleasant experience.

The leaders have several roles to play during a brainstorming session:

1. *They must introduce the problem.* It should be carefully worded so as to be perfectly clear and written for all to see on a board, easel, or overhead.

2. *They must appoint leaders and recorders of subgroups, if sub-groups are to be used, or indicate how the subgroups should choose their own leaders.*

3. *They must establish the ground rules suggested.* They need to encourage rapid-fire solutions while banning negatives comments or evaluations. They also need to encourage group members to present every idea that occurs.

4. *They must set the time limit.* They must also start and stop the discussion.

5. *They must caution those who are tempted to evaluate ideas prematurely.*

6. *They must call for suggested solutions from the recorder(s) and list them for all to see on a board, easel, or overhead.*

7. *They must lead the subsequent evaluation session.* This may be done by the whole group, by the subgroup leaders serving as a panel with reactions from the whole group following, or by a committee considering the solutions later.

The individual group member's roles will include (1) contributing intently, without restraint; (2) presenting any ideas they may think of; (3) hitchhiking on the ideas of others and adding to them, but not evaluating or negating them; (4) helping in the evaluation of ideas when called on to do so; and (5) sharing in determining a course of action if called on to do so.

Brainstorming should bring together people who are concerned with the problem. Their interest and concern will tend to make the session a success and serve their needs.

Many church and Christian education problems will yield to this method. For example: how to encourage interest in Sunday School; how to make the school a friendly school; how to promote stewardship; how to relate to or do more for youth, adults, senior citizens, etc.

Buzz Groups

Buzz groups function similarly to brainstorming, except comments are not necessarily rapid-fire and evaluation occurs as the group moves along in its consideration of the problem or idea. Buzz groups are small—three to six members—so as to allow maximum participation by each member. The technique is designed to draw out from the people involved their thoughts, ideas, feelings, and suggestions regarding the problem or idea.

Buzz groups differ from work groups in that the latter may convene in session after session, researching and consulting with resource people, etc., in between and during the sessions. In buzz groups, the participants provide and become involved with various resources.

The technique's values are likewise similar to those of brainstorming. Buzz groups allow for maximum participation by all members. It draws out shy members because the groups are small and all *must* share. Members build on each other's ideas, and usually the end product is a synthesis of all contributions. Thus, the session is stimulating and makes for a sense of accomplishment felt by all. This method is often used at the end of conferences or workshops to suggest follow-up action.

The technique is usually employed by a larger group breaking down into smaller groups and discussing the same issue or problem. At a set time the main group reconvenes and receives reports from each buzz group.

The leader's role is to (1) lead the group as it seeks to define and agree on the issue or problem to be discussed; (2) divide the group into buzz groups and name the leaders or tell how to select them; (3) give instructions concerning how the groups are to function in case some people have not used the technique before; (4) move from group to group acting in a resource capacity, checking and assisting as needed; (5) call time and reassemble the main group, calling for reports from each; (6) lead the discussion and evaluation session; (7) summarize the ideas and suggestions or the progress of the discussion; and (8) lead in the development of any conclusions and implementation of the action recommended.

Individual members function in roles similar to those of the brainstorming groups, except they are free to evaluate ideas as the discussion moves along. They (1) help state the issue or problem; (2) contribute in subgroups, defining the issue, giving suggestions, opinions, ideas, and helping to clarify and evaluate; (3) listen carefully to the ideas of others and react or respond; (4) help the group build toward its conclusions; (5) assist the main group as it reconvenes and evaluates each group's report; and (6) help determine how to implement the action agreed on.

The recorders in both the subgroups and the main group record the ideas, summarize them, and then report them. The summary and report are vital to the technique's success since the time advantage gained by having a number of groups operating at one time is retained through a brief report of each group's findings.

A true buzz group will usually last only five to eight minutes, depending on the nature of the question and the total time available. Simple questions can be handled in less time.

The buzz group should sit in a circle, with all its members facing each other. If several groups operate in one large room, the noise factor should be watched. However, the buzz of interaction and excited sharing of ideas can be stimulating and catch on.

Projects

It has already been established that telling is not teaching and hearing is not learning. Teaching is helping the student personalize truth. Learning is self-discovery of truth. Of the various levels of learning—listening, observation, vicarious experience, and direct experience—the latter is most effective. When learning is closely related to direct experience the probability that the learning will be meaningful and retained longer is greatly increased. One of the most effective ways to learn is by self-activity, by doing. The adage "Experience is the best teacher" is scientifically true.

Projects, which employ the principle of self-activity and allow the teacher to observe the students demonstrate the truth, can be of value for nearly any age. This technique provides the opportunity for the student to propose, plan, do the project, and evaluate both how it was done and what was done. Some materials can be taught more effectively by the project method than any other method, such as the many skills taught in a home economics class. Since the students learn by doing, they should never be given a meaningless activity.

Some of the values of this method include the following:

1. *The project may be done either in class or outside of class.*

2. *The project may be an individual, small-group, or whole-class activity.*

3. *Student motivation and interest are high.*

4. *The concepts being taught are related to life's experiences.*

5. *Skills are acquired while learning is taking place.*

6. *Responsibility for completion is vested in the students; thus, they learn stick-to-it-iveness, initiative, and cooperation.*

Findley Edge lists the following different types of projects in which a class may engage:

1. *Information projects lead class members to secure and master certain information.*

2. *Attitude projects change, develop, or deepen certain attitudes.*

3. *Habit projects develop certain desirable practices in the students' lives.*

4. *Service projects give expression to a Christian ideal that is accepted, to meet some need that is recognized, or to render service in some area.*[2]

In using the project method, the project should originate with the students. The activity should be of their choosing. It should grow out of their felt needs. After the project is chosen, the procedure should be planned. This too should be the students' work. The teacher's role should be that of an advisor, offering suggestions only when needed and helping the students to avoid making major errors.

When the project has been chosen and adequate planning has been done, the project should be carried through to its completion. This too should be the students' work. The teacher may coach, guide, advise, and counsel, but should not do the work for the students.

When the project is completed, the students should evaluate it. As the students rethink the process and the end product, they will recall the principles they have learned as they ask themselves, *What could we have done to avoid this problem?* or, *Why did we have success with this project?*

✳ ✳ ✳ ✳

Endnotes

1. Martha M. Leypoldt, *40 Ways To Teach in Groups* (Valley Forge, Pa.: Judson Press, 1967), 28.

2. Findley B. Edge, *Helping the Teacher* (Nashville, Tenn.: Broadman Press, 1959), 128–29.

✳7✳
Expressional Activities

One of the principles already studied is that learning is accomplished by doing. Each lesson should include some type of learning by doing. Such activities are not designed to fill the time until the bell rings. They are not a means of keeping little hands busy, but are intended to reinforce the lesson aim.

Expressional activities should be designed to lead the students to discover ways to implement the truth, to motivate and inspire them to integrate the truth into living, to help them discover how to make the carryover from lesson to life, and to implant the truth more deeply so it will be remembered longer. These activities should, therefore, be planned with the same care as the other parts of the lesson. Such learning should, like all learning, center in the students' interests, abilities, and needs.

Many such activities may be used. Here we shall consider only a few.

Interest/Learning Centers

Based on the principle of recognizing individual differences among students, the classroom is arranged to display various types of objects, pictures, or books that will reinforce the lesson aim by sensory contact. The centers may include a nature center, a creative-play area, a practical-life area, a listening area equipped with an audio system, a book center, etc.

At the beginning or the end of the class hour, or at some other point during the session, the students are permitted to move at will to the area that interests them. At each center is a teacher who is well briefed in the whole lesson and prepared to lead the learning experience in that center. The teacher reinforces the teaching aim by leading the students to discover the lesson truth from the viewpoint of the activity chosen by the students.

Learning centers bring many positive results to the teaching-learning situation. First, the variety of activities keeps interest high and discipline problems to a minimum. That enhances a good attitude toward Sunday School. Students who have interesting activities awaiting them each week look forward to Sunday School.

Second, the students learn to think for themselves. That helps them outside the classroom as well as in the class to develop Bible study skills and sharing.

Third, the value of choice and individualizing learning has already been touched on.

Fourth, the teacher benefits as well. Becoming a guide at an interest or learning center is an excellent way for a beginning teacher to develop a teaching ministry.

Ideally, a large open area should be used for learning centers. However, a large assembly room with smaller classrooms surrounding it can also work effectively. Even small classrooms leading from a central hall could be used.

Learning centers work well with very young children, but each center must always be staffed. When using learning centers for older children or adults it is practical, even desirable, to include some unmanned centers with written instructions for individual work.

Basic equipment for learning centers includes tables and chairs, shelving, art easels, bulletin boards, housekeeping supplies and blocks for preschool areas, books, maps, pictures, magazines, CDs, DVDs, tapes, sheet and roll paper, art supplies, modeling clay, crayons, felt-tipped pens, scissors, etc.

Audiovisual equipment, such as CD and DVD players, televisions, video projectors, and computers, are valuable resources, but are not essential. In fact, most churches could begin using learning centers with the equipment they already have.

The learning-center approach works best within a two-hour session, but can be used when less time is available. Several scheduling options are possible:

1. *Use learning centers throughout the entire session. During this time the students work with the activities of their choice. This works well with younger preschool children.*

2. *Have the students rotate from one center to another according to a predetermined schedule.*

3. *Use whole-department activities for part of the session.* The class or department may meet together for music, storytelling, and worship, then move to learning centers for memory work, handwork, research, playtime, etc.[1]

It is best to begin the learning-center program with one department at a time. Parents and students, as well as teachers, need to be oriented to the learning-center approach.

Games

Capitalize on the students' sense of adventure and competition by using games. Games can be used to review (e.g., Bible baseball, basketball, football, etc.) or to teach important spiritual concepts, such as honesty and teamwork.

Be creative in the games you choose to teach lesson truths. With children, a game of Simon Says can teach the importance of obeying rules. Older children and adults can benefit from a game of Bible charades or Pictionary (drawing clues). If you're looking for great ways to capture the attention of youth and adults, keep abreast of games that are currently popular and adapt the concepts of one so that it will teach key lesson truths.

Fingerplays and Action Rhymes

Combining one of the small child's favorite pastimes with learning, use simple rhymes coupled with finger or large-muscle actions to settle restless little ones, prepare them for a story, prayer time, or a rest period. These simple exercises, often described in preschool teachers manuals, arrest attention, reinforce the Bible lesson by acting it out, make learning fun and memorable, provide opportunity for muscle stretching and body movement, and tend to fix ideas in young minds.

Freehand Expressive Art

It is a fact that some students learn better visually than verbally. Therefore, it is important to provide art activities with regularity and purpose. Some students may balk at expressing themselves through art, but persevere. Most dissatisfaction comes from a fear of failing. Keep a warm and accepting climate and most students will come around and enjoy creative expression. Some will even thrive on art.

Expressive art gets students to sum up their thoughts and ideas about the subject and weave them into projects that express the students in very personal ways. Always commend their real efforts and never belittle their results. Consider using art in some of the following ways: banners, posters, graffiti posters, illustrating the lesson for children, sculpture, ripped-paper designs, symbolic art (e.g., "Draw something that represents home to you"), painting, caricatures, cartoon strips, etc. The list is endless. Use your imagination to think up new possibilities and tailor them to your lesson objective.

Creative Writing

Once again, you may need to help the students over their initial reluctance to express themselves creatively. You may want to lead up to writing by giving them creative tasks to complete verbally. They will soon discover the value of writing down their work and become more comfortable with expressing themselves.

Here is a brief list of creative writing projects:

1. *Scripture paraphrase*—Have students rewrite, in their own words, a Scripture passage used in the day's lesson. This ensures that the students think about and really understand the Bible text.

2. *News stories*—This writing technique is designed to acquaint the students with the biblical account in light of how it would be reported in today's local newspaper. Encourage the students to be factual but creative as they answer the basic questions: who, what, when, where, why, and how. Sometimes it may be appropriate to assign a feature article in which the students explore the actions and feelings of characters in the story.

3. *Diary entries*—Closely related to news stories are diary

entries. Allow the students to choose a character and write an account of what happened to him or her in relation to a specific biblical event (e.g., the day after the walls of Jericho fell, or the day before Jesus's resurrection).

4. *Parables*—Parable writing often reveals exceptional student insight as well as creativity. Instruct the students to write a true-to-life story illustrating a specific lesson truth. Fable writing employs the same concept, but a fable need not be true to life. Usually fables feature fictional animal characters who talk or learn lessons. Be sure to use this method only with students who are old enough to recognize the assignment's purpose and fictional nature.

There are many other creative ideas to consider. Why not have the students write travelogues or brochures about the Bible area being studied? Or ask them to write their own tracts to use as witnessing tools. Try having each student write a devotional piece to add to a class booklet. Or how about assigning an acrostic in which a descriptive word is listed for each letter of a key word, such as *patience*?

Don't hesitate to assign students to write poetry. Most students love limericks. Or how about alphabet poetry, in which each alphabet letter begins its own line? As you can see, the possibilities are limitless.

Creative Drama

Drama, traditionally considered an art, has in recent times come to be recognized as a creative means of learning. Lease and Siks define creative drama as "a group activity in which meaningful experience is acted out by the participants as they create their own dialogue and action."[2]

Creative drama, sometimes referred to as educational drama or playmaking, is commonly used as a general term for any kind of play that utilizes the imagination, the great world of "let's pretend." The children express their innermost feelings in action.

The basic purpose of this approach is to develop the learner, not to produce plays. The process is important, rather than the product. Student participation is desired above a finished production. Since student involvement is the key, there need be no audience, although on some occasions part of the class may act out a part for their peers to observe and evaluate. What child hasn't enjoyed playing house with no audience to look on! Likewise, only the simplest scenery, costumes, staging, etc., should be used—if any at all.

The values of creative drama are educational, recreational, devotional, cultural, and therapeutic. As a conflict that requires a decision of right or wrong is dramatized, character and values are taught. This teaching method helps the students gain self-confidence and self-understanding, helps them win others' acceptance, and teaches appreciation of others.

Recognizing the differences of individual students, creative drama teaches creativity, develops self-expression, and leads to the realization that the Christian faith is a vital living reality. As the players identify with the characters, the events become so vivid to both players and observers that all have the feelings of sharing in the experience. Thus they not only remember the facts, but also enter into the feelings of the situation.

With a few adaptations, this learning activity can be appropriate for any elementary-age child. Through creative drama, education in the church is kept similar to life in the home; thus, children are on familiar ground and tend to be more secure.

Let us consider the many types of creative drama:

1. *Plays include several types:*
    a. The formal play is characterized by definite actions and

memorized dialogue, and is prepared for public presentation. Such plays require staging, costumes, scenery, etc.

b. In the informal play, the actions and dialogue are extemporaneous rather than written and memorized. The players act out the events, making up their own words and actions as they go.

c. In the original play, the students create the plot, dialogue, and action in advance. They then memorize these and produce the play. It is their original work. While the process is time-consuming, it can be very effectively used to dramatize a problem or to present a present-day version of a Bible narrative.

d. The story play or story drama is undoubtedly the most popular type of play for educational use. The students assume the role of the characters in a Bible story and act out the story.

2. *Pantomimes are simple reenactments of an action scene, using body movements and facial expressions but no words.* The players only act. The teacher, or another student, may tell or read the story as the players silently dramatize it. Shy students may gain self-confidence and become creative in self-expression as they participate in a Bible pantomime.

3. *Shadow pictures, a form of pantomime, are the acting out of a story behind a screen.* Again, the actors do not speak. Simple costumes may prove valuable, but are generally not required. The screen can easily be made by suspending a sheet in front of a corner of the room and placing a spotlight far enough back to permit the players to act between the light and the screen. As in the pantomime, a narrator tells or reads the story as it is being acted out.

4. *Pageants are reenactments of historical events.* Costuming and appropriate staging are thus appropriate. Christianity affords many such opportunities, such as Christmas or Passion Week pageants.

5. *The tableau, a picture without words or actions, can effectively portray a problem or present new insights into a situation.* The actors form the scene and dramatize the idea without words or movements.

6. *Puppets, inanimate objects used to act out the story or truth being taught, attract attention to themselves and away from the players.* Puppets may be used by the teacher or the students. The students, especially the self-conscious, tend to lose themselves in healthy emotional release while using puppets. As the puppets dramatize the story, it is fixed in the students' minds in a fashion that is exciting and fun.

   There are many kinds of puppets, including paper-bag puppets, mitten puppets, sock puppets, hand puppets, finger puppets and stick puppets, to list just a few.

7. *Role playing is a general term that refers to the spontaneous acting out of roles in the context of human-relations situations.* Educationally, it is a technique by which members of a group act out roles, functions, and emotional overtones of a problem-solving situation dealing with interpersonal relationships. There are two basic types of role playing.

   a. The sociodrama deals with the interactions of people with individuals or groups in some specific cultural role. It involves more than one person and deals with problems faced by the majority of the group.

   b. The psychodrama deals with unique, individual, personal problems that are of an emotional nature. It therefore is a form of group therapy and should be attempted only under the guidance of a trained therapist. Further reference to the general term, role playing, will be limited in meaning to the sociodrama.

Bearing many similarities to creative drama, role playing is spontaneous, unrehearsed, and has no specific plot. It can be used most effectively with older youth and adults.

By acting out normal or problematic human-relations situations, opportunity is given for the students to objectively discuss situations that would be too emotionally charged to handle in real life. The students may discuss attitudes that would not normally be expressed as they actively engage in the teaching-learning process.

While observing the role play, the students may come to better understand how others feel and why they act as they do. They may see themselves more clearly and discover methods of working out solutions to their problems. Role plays tend to take the students inside their own as well as other people's feelings to gain an understanding and appreciation of them. Care should be taken, however, to avoid overpersonalization of problems.

It is wise, therefore, especially with self-conscious teens, to separate the actors from the fictional characters. That can be done by writing the characters' names on nametags or pieces of paper and pinning or taping them to the actors. Then in follow-up discussion, negative comments should be directed at the character and not at the students personally.

After the scene is chosen and the characters are briefed, the role play is presented, usually lasting no longer than five to seven minutes. Only the problem should be presented. The action must be cut at that point. The solutions should result from the group discussion that follows.

Six basic steps should be followed in using creative drama in teaching:

1. *Information*—The students cannot create in a vacuum. They must know the story well. This information may be gained by telling, reading, or research.

2. *Discussion*—As the group members talk it through, they engage in mental activity to prepare for the next step.

3. *Decision*—The students decide how to present the drama.

4. *Planning*—The students list the various alternatives and evaluate each one. Learning is genuinely taking place here.

5. *Production*—Remember the quality of product is not as important as what happens to the students. An audience is not needed to receive maximum teaching value.

6. *Evaluation*—The players, again themselves and no longer characters, are ready to face the truth of the pretend situation. They should think through the process even though they may not talk it through. This is a highly personal time, and some students may think honestly about the moral presented, but not want to reveal their innermost secrets.

Since creative drama is a group learning activity, the teacher lays a more passive role. The students are central while the teacher is an advisor, counselor, and guide who assists them discovering truth from their own creativity.

Learning without proper reinforcement is apt to be short of the depth that is needed to make the transfer from lesson to life. Plan for expressional activities; experiment and be amazed the difference in your class.

✳ ✳ ✳ ✳

Endnotes

1. Ronald G. Held, *Learning Together* (Springfield, Mo.: Gospel Publishing House, 1976), 53.

2. Ruth Lease and Geraldine Brain Siks, *Creative Dramatics in Home, School and Community* (New York: Harper & Brothers, 1952), 3.

8

Audiovisual Benefits

The beginning teacher would do well to think about using audiovisual aids right from the start.

Variety of Audiovisuals

Many forms of audiovisuals are used and available: the board, PowerPoint, overhead projectors, video projectors, cassette tapes, videotape, CDs, DVDs, computers, flashcards, visuals, posters, maps, objects, puppets, etc. Each has its particular advantage and is adaptable to various age-levels. All do much to hold attention and illustrate ideas.

Most lesson materials (including Radiant Life) have visual and audio aids prepared to accompany them or suggest some the teacher may make. Exerting the extra effort necessary to incorporate visual and audio aids is always worthwhile. The dividends reaped in class response and learning accomplishment will be gratifying. Visual aids may be placed in several categories:

1. *Prepared visuals*—Flannelgraph figures, posters, flashcards,

and other preprinted items specifically designed to go with a lesson have distinct advantages. Usually they are age-level accurate and prepared specifically for the purpose at hand. The visuals can stimulate interest and hold attention if handled properly. Teachers should prepare beforehand so that their use of the visuals is appropriate and goes smoothly.

Teachers should be aware that when they turn their backs to place visuals on a flannelboard behind them, they momentarily break contact with the students and stand a greater chance of losing their attention. You can remedy this by keeping the board in front of you while you continue to face the students.

Use visuals creatively. Consider allowing students to make or place the visuals. Or have a student use visuals to review the story. Get additional use out of visuals by posting them around the room as decorations and continual reminders of the lesson.

Visuals are not just for children. Teachers should not overlook the value of a poster, photo, or illustration when attempting to bring home a point to youth or adults.

2. *The board*—More teachers use this universal visual help than all other visuals, and rightly so. It is easily used, versatile, and requires a minimum of preparation. Every Christian education classroom should have one mounted on the wall and available for use at all times.

Many teachers hesitate to make full use of the board because they lack experience. Actually, however, those who use their hands as they talk or who use a pencil and a piece of paper to make meanings clear can use a board. All teachers need to do is keep the chalk or dry erase marker handy. Eventually they will discover they are using it without giving much thought to it. At times they may plan to use it in explaining a series of points or a brief outline. Sometimes simply one word or a symbol will suffice. Teachers' first attempts may seem awkward, but they

106

will improve if they keep practicing.

The best use of the board is spontaneous and free, on the impulse of the moment. A simple diagram placed on the board can symbolize an involved and detailed concept. A brief reference to the symbol calls back the entire concept without restatement by the teacher. Thus symbols, maps, words, etc., placed on the board are a track of the lesson, or a portion of it, and serve as visual reminders of what has been said.

3. *The overhead projector*—This teaching help is quite versatile. Because it throws its picture onto a screen, the teacher can face the audience while writing or pointing to material on the projector. The overhead has the added advantage that the teacher can make transparencies before class.

Professional quality transparencies can be purchased through Gospel Publishing House. Those featuring maps or other historical data are excellent resources for teaching Bible history.

Many other avenues are open for obtaining good transparencies. Teachers may make their own, specifically tailoring them to the exact lesson and point to be taught. Be sure, however, that the publisher has granted permission for you to make copies for classroom use. Overheads need not be fancy to be effective. Lined paper (or quadrille grid paper for art) should be used as a guide when making transparencies or, if possible, use a computer and printer.

Also, most copy shops have the equipment to copy any printed material onto a transparency. Take advantage of this technology, but be sure to choose copy that will be large enough to be read from a distance away.

4. *Cassette tapes/CDs*—Cassette tapes, CDs, and players are common, inexpensive, and small enough to take anywhere. The possibilities are endless. Consider playing appropriate music, drama, interviews, or dialogue. You may keep it simple

or get creative, adding sound effects, music, and using different voices.

Using the equipment to record during class is also recommended. It is helpful to any teacher to record an entire class to evaluate performance. In addition, consider involving students in projects using the recorder. Have them read a skit on tape while others make sound effects. Or, interview students on tape at the beginning of a unit or year and then play the tape at the end so they may see how their attitudes and situations have changed. Be creative. There are many excellent uses for the cassette tape.

5. *Camcorders*—Most camcorders are easy to operate, can play back immediately on a standard television with VCR or DVD, and offer endless possibilities for the contemporary teacher. This method is excellent for allowing students to do creative interviews, commercials for spiritual concepts, skits and drama, and demonstrations. Videotape can also bring guests who would otherwise never be able to come to your classroom.

Remember also, appropriate professional teaching tapes and DVDs may be purchased or rented for viewing in your class.

6. *Videos/DVDs*—These should be a part of the total teaching program, used to facilitate learning, and not ends in themselves. They should be used to reinforce lessons, not serve as a substitute for teaching. Be sure to preview the movie carefully to avoid unpleasant surprises. Also, prepare an introduction; include the movie's purpose and value to the group and specific things to watch for. Always follow up the movie with a time of discussion or feedback; otherwise, the students tend to be spectators. Discussion encourages personalization of the lesson.

7. *PowerPoint*—Computer based programs combined with

video projectors provide a wide range of opportunities for teachers. These programs allow teachers to create presentations that combine animation and sound to appeal to a variety of learning styles.

The drawback to video projection is the cost of equipment. Although the costs continue to fall as the technology increases, most churches can't afford to have equipment for every classroom. It is recommended that churches purchase portable models and establish a "check-out" policy so teachers can schedule the equipment in an equitable manner.

8. *Maps*—These should be available and used much more often than they are. Teachers should consult maps in advance, find locations, and be prepared to point them out. Relationships are important to learning and retention. A Bible lands map is always a vital teaching tool.

In the lower age-levels, a profitable technique is to ask the students to locate the cities or areas about which you are learning. It may take time, but the students are learning while doing it.

Conclusion

Although audiovisuals are valuable teaching helps, the teacher must be careful to make sure the audiovisuals serve the purpose of the lesson. Using visuals just for the sake of maintaining interest or to entertain may result in a failure to teach. Even the most exciting audiovisual cannot replace a competent, caring teacher in the classroom.

✳ ✳ ✳ ✳

✻ 9 ✻

Effective Lesson Preparation

The importance of careful lesson preparation cannot be overvalued or overemphasized. It is indispensable to effective teaching. As teachers prepare their lessons, God ministers truth to them so they can effectively minister to the students. When the teachers are enriched, the students are enriched.

In planning the lesson, the teacher determines how to use the time wisely, deciding what to include in the lesson and what to exclude. The teacher establishes the lesson aims and plans the means of achieving them. The teacher can then anticipate the class hour with a sense of security and confidence. Teaching God's Word is far too sacred a ministry for the teacher to fail to prepare adequately.

Lesson preparation requires time, energy, talent, and commitment. Yet the rewards are more than adequate payment for the effort. The joy of being a co-worker with God in building lives and fulfilling the mission of the Church is great indeed. The lasting friendships and relationships that are built with students and their families provide rich rewards;

not to mention the anticipated sound of the Master's, "Well done thou good and faithful servant."

Effective Preparation Techniques

Lesson preparation fits into two categories:

1. *General lesson preparation is the sum total of the teacher's background.* The whole of life's experiences, a growing knowledge of the Bible and Church doctrine, familiarity with people's age-level needs, and an understanding of teaching-learning techniques all fit into this category.

2. *Specific lesson preparation is the careful, detailed planning for next Sunday's lesson.* That will provide the basis of our study in the remainder of the lesson.

Lesson preparation should be as much teacher preparation as anything. Teachers must be ready spiritually, emotionally, and intellectually, if they are to communicate God's Word. Specific lesson preparation involves two aspects: (1) spiritual and (2) practical. To be spiritually ready for the classroom, the teacher must maintain a growing relationship with Christ that is fostered in personal devotional Bible study and prayer. The value of this cannot be overstressed.

Lesson preparation should begin as soon as the teacher receives the materials for the next quarter's lessons.

The first step is a quick preview of the entire quarter's work. Along with a quick reading of the teachers and students manuals, all related Scripture passages should be carefully read. The preview process will help the teacher to understand the entire series, to gain insight into the background of the series, and to be on the lookout for appropriate supplementary materials and audio-visuals.

The preview process will also enable the teacher to establish

112

objectives for the entire quarter. The objectives should be carefully formulated and written down for quick and easy reference. Most quarterly studies contain two or three units, which should be identified and their relationship to the entire quarter's studies determined. Aims for each individual lesson should then be written down.

Establishing and writing aims is the second step of lesson planning. All other effort is futile until the direction of the lesson has been set by establishing aims that take into account the students' specific needs. Each lesson aim should build toward the unit's and quarter's aims, so that proper progress will be made.

Educational change occurs in three areas: knowledge, attitude, and conduct. Since objectives are the anticipated changes, these areas will form the framework for your objectives. If the purpose of the lesson is to impart information and facts that will lead to a mastery of the Bible, your objective should be a knowledge objective. If the purpose is to change an attitude, deepen appreciation, or stimulate some desired feeling, your objective should be an attitude aim. If the purpose is to call for action, behavioral change, or response in changed living, your objective should be a conduct aim.

While developing a specific objective may call for more detailed thinking, the teacher must focus the aim very carefully and avoid the temptation to be too general or broad.

Although a Scripture passage may lend itself to several different aims, each lesson should be prepared with only one aim in view. One arrow won't hit several targets. That means some lessons may not end with an appeal for the students to do anything; the aim is only to impart knowledge. Another lesson may not relate any new knowledge at all; the aim is to act on what is already known or to think and feel the way one already knows one should.

The following questions will help determine what aim

to select for the lesson under study:

1. *What is the major truth being taught in the passage?* Usually the teachers manual will suggest an objective, but the teachers must adapt or modify it to meet their students' unique needs.

2. *How does the Scripture passage relate to my students' particular needs?* The teacher must know the personal needs of each student. Usually a student's questions and comments during class will give the perceptive teacher insight into the student.

3. *In the passage, what is the Holy Spirit saying about my students' needs?* As you pray about the lesson and for your students, you may sense that God is speaking to you about a particular aspect of the lesson or a particular problem. That will become the basis of your emphasis in the lesson. Be open to God's leading. Expect Him to speak to you as you seek Him on behalf of your class.

4. *To what kind of aim does the Scripture passage best lend itself?* Does it primarily impart facts or deal with attitudes or conduct?

An example of each type of objective, written on the teenage level, is as follows:

Knowledge
Scripture passage: John 1:1–14.
Aim: To understand that Jesus is the God-Man.

Attitude
Scripture passage: Psalm 119.
Aim: To appreciate and love the Bible, God's Word.

Conduct
Scripture passage: Acts 5:1–10.
Aim: To tell the truth at all times.

Most teachers manuals provide a general objective, which

you may or may not use. Obviously the writer of the manual, while knowing well the characteristics of the age-level being taught, does not know your students' individual needs. But you do know those needs and can write aims that will meet them. If you use the aim stated in the manual, you will need to add the specifics to it. For example, the conduct aim mentioned above might appear in the manual, but you would have to add the specifics: to not cheat on the exam in school, to tell the truth about who was the first to invite Johnny to the Sunday School contest, etc.

Each week, as the teacher begins to prepare for the following Sunday, the aim for that lesson should be clearly in focus. All of the planning from that point on should be to fulfill that objective. Each step of the lesson should play a vital part in achieving the aim.

The third step in lesson preparation is gathering the material. The teacher should carefully read both the teachers and students manuals. However, the teachers manual should never be read to the class; it is only a study tool for the teacher. The helps it provides should be used as such. It is in no wise the only source of information from which the teacher should glean material. Material should be gathered from many other sources. Tools that teachers should have readily available include (1) a good one-volume Bible commentary, (2) a Bible atlas, (3) a Bible dictionary, (4) a Bible concordance (5) a book on the customs of Bible times, and (6) a doctrine or theology textbook.

These tools are basic to every teacher's study and research and should be purchased as soon as possible.

As the teacher reads from such sources, usable ideas and other materials will begin to come to mind. Ideas should be written down immediately so they will not be forgotten. Many teachers keep a notebook for their lesson preparation. Poems, illustrations, ideas, and ways to communicate the material all go into the notebook.

Teachers should always gather more material than they expect to use in any single lesson. While gathering material, find answers to the following questions:

1. *Who are the persons in the biblical account?*

2. *Who was the writer?*

3. *When was the passage written?*

4. *Under what conditions was it written?*

5. *To whom was it addressed?*

6. *Why was it addressed to them?*

Try to determine what the writer had in mind. Attempt to determine just what is being said and what those to whom it was written understood it to mean. Study the material to master its content without attempting to devotionalize at this point. Look up any words or idioms to discover their meaning. Your research will undoubtedly call for rereading the passage many times as well as reading the context of several chapters or possibly the entire book.

The fourth step is assembling the material. With the aim clearly in mind, the material will begin to relate itself around certain basic ideas. Write down a working outline of the material. As you ponder the ideas they will likely become the major points of the outline and the rest of the material you have gathered will be supporting evidence.

As the ideas begin to work themselves together into an outline, carefully plan the introduction and conclusion, giving equal care to the main body of the lesson. It will also be necessary to plan the transitions from one part to another. Each step should further develop the one main goal of the lesson, with a smooth transition from point to point, maintaining the students' interest.

The fifth step in lesson preparation is selecting the method. Now that the teacher has accumulated and organized all the material, the question should be asked: *How can I best communicate this material to my students?* All the methods that have been studied in recent lessons are available to the teacher, but since they cannot all be used in any single lesson, how can the best methods be discovered?

As a general rule, every lesson should use more than one method. The following tests will help you decide what methods to use in a particular lesson:

1. *Aim test*—Which methods will best help accomplish the lesson's aim?

2. *Time test*—Can I economically use the method in the time available for the lesson?

3. *Age test*—Is the method suitable for my students' interests and age?

4. *Background test*—Do the students have adequate background to use the method to its fullest?

5. *Content test*—Is the method suited to communicating this lesson?

6. *Equipment-facility test*—Can it be used with the facilities and equipment available to me? Will it work in our classroom?

7. *Needs test*—Will the method meet the students' needs?

8. *Size of class test*—Is the method feasible in view of the number of students in my class?

9. *Involvement test*—Will using the method result in student participation in the teaching-learning process?

10. *Aptitude test*—Does the method demand too little or too much of the students' skills or of my skills?

11. *Variety test*—Have I recently used the method? Am I overusing it?

12. *Growth test*—Will using it lead to spiritual growth in my students? Will it lead them to want to discover truth and include that truth in their daily living?

In planning the method, the teacher should have the entire class session in focus. Teaching should begin when the first student arrives. A planned activity introducing the lesson aim should be available. As the students continue to arrive, they should be included in the activity.

The lesson should then proceed to a group activity that will present the day's theme and get thinking started on the aim you have selected. You are then ready for the main body of the lesson, which may be presented in small-group settings or to the entire class, depending on the purpose and the methods chosen. The lesson time should end with an expressional activity. The students should begin to express in their daily lives the truth of the lesson.

The class session will probably include a worship time, which may come near the beginning, at the end, or at some point in between. The songs, prayer, Bible verses, devotionals, etc., should be carefully planned to tie in with the lesson theme and reinforce the learning aim.

The teacher will want to plan the room arrangement as well. Different methods call for different arrangements. When possible it is best for the learners to be situated so they can see one another. Varying the room arrangement from week to week, as it is set up in different ways for different presentations, can make a small room seem larger.

If the presentation calls for projected visuals, be sure the screen is in place and the ventilation and temperature controlled. Place the chairs so that all the students will be able to see well. Take into consideration the glare produced by the sun shining through the windows. If the lesson calls for interest centers, plan them carefully and set them up in advance. If the lesson calls for movement by the students, be sure the furniture is back against the walls.

Lighting can be a major factor in contributing to good learning. The teacher should see that burned-out bulbs are promptly replaced and that there is adequate light in the room to read comfortably without eyestrain.

Obviously there is much to bear in mind when selecting the method. Since it will be the core of the lesson, no details should be ignored.

The sixth step in lesson preparation is writing out the lesson plan. That is the instrument the teacher will take into the classroom. It should include statements about everything that will happen in the class session, with the time allotted for each.

All teachers develop their own style of lesson plan. Some teachers prefer to write out an entire manuscript, others a sentence outline, some a word or phrase outline, while others use only notes. However it is done, the lesson plan should be convenient, easy to use, and thorough. Once it is written it should be followed to avoid any number of a host of embarrassing situations. When the Holy Spirit has led the teacher all week long in preparing the lesson, the lesson plan becomes a valuable tool in effecting the ministry with the class.

The final step in lesson preparation is review. After the whole process is complete the information should be reread several times. Go over the Scripture portions and any illustrations you plan to use. Rethink the methods you have chosen. If you began your planning early enough in the week, you should be able to spend an hour or so on Saturday going over what you have prepared. Then you will be ready to approach the classroom with confidence and ease, rather than attempting to do all the planning late Saturday evening or early Sunday morning. Teaching is a God-given ministry and, therefore, deserves our very best in preparation.

On Sunday afternoon, following the class period, evaluate the session. Write down any questions that were asked, particularly any questions for which you did not have a ready answer. Be honest with yourself in this evaluation. No lesson is ever so perfect that it could stand no improvement. Ask yourself, How can I improve for next time?

✳ ✳ ✳ ✳

Sample Lesson Plan for a Teenage Class

QUARTER'S THEME: God's Faithfulness

QUARTER'S AIM: To help the students realize how great and faithful God is

LESSON THEME: God's faithfulness in hearing and answering prayer

SCRIPTURE PASSAGE: 1 Kings 3:5–14

MAJOR TRUTH TAUGHT IN PASSAGE: God heard and answered Solomon's prayer.

STUDENTS' NEEDS TO BE MET BY THIS LESSON:
1. To feel confident that God hears our prayers
2. To realize that God is powerful enough to answer our prayers
3. To discover the value of prayer in our personal lives

LESSON AIM: Knowledge—to realize that God hears and answers the prayers of His obedient children

LESSON PLAN

BEFORE CLASS BEGINS: Presession—Have each student write a short paragraph telling about a recent prayer God has answered.

FIVE MINUTES: Have a few volunteers read the paragraphs they wrote giving testimony of God's answers to their prayers.

TEN MINUTES: Storytelling time—Tell the story contained in the Scripture passage, introducing the lesson theme and aim.

FIVE MINUTES: Scripture memorization (James 5:16)

FIFTEEN MINUTES: Divide the class into small groups of three to five, depending on how many are present, and give the following assignments:

121

Group one: Using a concordance, discover how many times prayer is mentioned in the Bible.

Group two: Using a Bible dictionary, discover the meaning of prayer.

Group three: Study the Lord's Prayer to discover the method of prayer.

TEN MINUTES: Have each group report back to the class.

FIVE MINUTES: Have students write requests for which they will pray throughout the week. Let it be a personal matter. Do not ask to see what the students write.

TEN MINUTES: Worship time—Have the class join in singing "Great Is Thy Faithfulness, O God, Our Father," which is the theme song for the quarter.

PRAYER TIME: Lead prayer, praying for the requests the students have written and asking God to help the class understand that He answers prayer.

* 10 *

Practice Teaching and Evaluation

Now that the student teachers have completed a broad basis of classroom training and have observed experienced teachers in the teaching task, it is time to practice teach. Teaching skills, like most other skills, can best be learned by doing.

The student teachers must be allowed to teach if the principles they have learned are to become a part of their ministries. Just as the medical student interns under the supervision of a licensed doctor, and the education major practice teaches under the supervision of a certified teacher, so the Sunday School student teacher should practice teach under the supervision of an experienced Sunday School teacher. Since practice teaching is a learning experience, the student teachers should do their practice teaching under the supervision of veteran teachers, even though to do so may be more difficult.

The supervising teachers should not see this as an opportunity to vacation from their classes. Instead they should view it as an opportunity to further expand their ministries by having a part in the ministry of a student teacher.

123

Often various pressures allow for only one formal practice-teaching experience—that should be considered minimal. The student teachers would do well to work with experienced teachers for several weeks before being appointed to classes of their own.

Practice teaching offers many values to the student teachers, the Sunday School, the supervising teacher, and the students:

1. *To the student teachers*—Undoubtedly the greatest values are to the student teachers as they are introduced to the problems and challenges of the teaching ministry, face students firsthand, gain confidence, try their skills, and receive the counsel and evaluation of the supervising teachers.

2. *To the school*—The school receives the benefits of having prospective teachers who have had at least minimal teaching experience. That should result in a corps of teaching candidates who are more secure and less frustrated, resulting in fewer vacant teaching positions.

3. *To the supervising teachers*—While there will be no less preparation for the supervising teachers, they will benefit by being forced to sharpen their skills to adequately supervise the student teachers by engaging in the process of evaluation, and by seeing how another teaches. And the supervising teachers may gain value from the student teachers' research and new methodologies.

The student teachers should observe certain basics before, during, and after the teaching experience.

✳ ✳ ✳ ✳

Assignment for Student Teaching

Before the class:

	I Did	I Didn't
1. Review the age-level characteristics of the group to be taught.	_____	_____
2. Become familiar with the individual needs of the students by a conference with the supervising teacher.	_____	_____
3. Learn the goals the supervising teacher has established for the class for the year and quarter.	_____	_____
4. Determine how the lesson to be taught fits into that pattern.	_____	_____
5. Familiarize yourself with any class rules of conduct, etc., that the supervising teacher may have established.	_____	_____
6. Acquaint yourself with the nature of other classes, how the supervising teacher conducts the average class, etc.	_____	_____
7. Familiarize yourself with the room environment, facilities, and equipment available. If necessary, rearrange the room for the intended use in the lesson.	_____	_____
8. Plan the lesson carefully.	_____	_____
9. Determine and understand the objective.	_____	_____
10. Have adequate materials ready.	_____	_____

During the class:

	I Did	I Didn't
1. Show enthusiasm.	_____	_____
2. Get off to a good start.	_____	_____
3. Demonstrate confidence and competence.	_____	_____

	I Did	I Didn't
4. Use the students' ideas.	_____	_____
5. Keep your sense of humor.	_____	_____
6. Keep the students' attention centered on the class activity.	_____	_____
7. Help the students see the relationship of the lesson to life and help them apply the lesson correctly.	_____	_____
8. Plan for expressional activity. Don't do it all yourself. Involve the students in the teaching-learning process.	_____	_____
9. Keep ahead of the students. Anticipate their questions and doubts, and attempt to answer them.	_____	_____
10. Stick to it. Don't give up or become frustrated if all does not go as planned.	_____	_____

After the class:

Evaluate the teaching experience.   _____   _____

Evaluation

The practice-teaching experience is primarily to be a learning experience. To be of maximum value, the experience must be evaluated. Likewise, the evaluation process should be a learning situation. It therefore should be consistent with the goals of practice teaching; should analyze the progress that was made; should be informal, cooperative, and specific; and should provide for both self-evaluation and evaluation from the supervising teacher.

There are several reasons for evaluating the student-teaching experience:

1. *To help the student teachers analyze their teaching experiences*

2. *To allow the student teachers to profit from the supervising teachers' observations*

3. *To help the student teachers see themselves more clearly*

4. *To help the student teachers overcome frustrations that may have developed*

5. *To assist the student teachers in becoming more efficient teachers*

6. *To help the student teachers think creatively about the problems they should anticipate as they becomes regular teachers*

7. *To cause the student teachers to think creatively about solutions to problems that may have come up in their teaching experiences*

8. *To get the student teachers started in the task of evaluating their own teaching*

Evaluation Review

The process of evaluation includes setting goals, gathering evidence, interpreting the evidence, formulating conclusions, and making recommendations. Since the goals for the teaching experience will already be established, it will be necessary only to reread and rethink the goals. The gathering of evidence will include asking a series of questions and thinking about certain items which will be mentioned later. It will be valuable to complete a checklist similar to the observation forms included in the appendix.

While the evaluation should basically be the task of the student teacher, the supervising teacher should also submit information that should be considered. The conclusions drawn should not be of the type, *I am going to be a good teacher or I am a failure as a teacher*. Instead, the conclusions should include a listing of both the advantages and limitations of the teaching session. Recommendations should include what may be done to improve the limitations and enhance the advantages.

Since the student teacher is endeavoring to both teach and

learn, the relationship between the student teacher and the supervising teacher is complex and doubly sensitive. Probably at no point is this relationship more strained than in the evaluation process. The interpersonal relationship must be controlled by Christian attitudes, to say the least. Each must believe that the other has the other's best interests at heart.

The student teachers must be given opportunities to exercise their ministries while under the careful observation of supervising teachers. The supervisors must allow the students to be creative and do things differently than the supervisors might be used to doing.

Supervision calls for patience, perception, and skill. The student teachers should make every effort to understand the supervisors' viewpoints. Thus, as practice teachers and supervisors think and evaluate together, much value can result.

Evaluation should be the result of continuous thinking rather than a single event. The process may include listing the experiences the student teachers feel were helpful in preparing them for their own classes. They may also want to list the experiences that need improvement. The student teachers should think about what could have been done in their lesson planning that would have corrected some of the problems.

Some problems may be caused by a personality factor within the teacher which will call for long-range correction by continually working on the problem. Student teachers should list the strengths and weaknesses of their own personal characters as prospective teachers.

It would also be appropriate to consider the students' reactions to the student teachers. If students' reactions were favorable, the student teachers should try to determine why. If reactions were unfavorable, the student teachers should try to determine what could be done to overcome those reactions.

Finally, the student teachers should compare the remarks

made by the supervising teachers, the students, and their own reactions to the situations. They should list the most often repeated virtues at the top and grade the rest downward, then do likewise with the problem areas. Each practice teacher should ask: *Why did I say that? Why did I use that activity? Was that activity in the best economy of time for the goals set? How did the students view the activity?*

Evaluation is not a simple or an easy process, but the student teacher would be wise to begin to evaluate each teaching session.

✳ ✳ ✳ ✳

Appendix
Observation of Teaching

Option 1

1. What aspects of the central message of the gospel were stressed in the class session?

   _____

   _____

   _____

   _____

2. What methods, as viewed briefly in relation to Jesus's teaching, were used in the session?

   _____

   _____

3. What was the main method employed?

   _____

   _____

4. Observe the teacher's motivation and comment on it.

   _____

   _____

5. What evidences of learning taking place were present?

   _____

   _____

6. What could have been done to intensify the learning accomplishment, either by the students or the teacher?

   _____

   _____

7. How did the teacher seek to motivate the learning?

_____

_____

   a. Was the whole experience well planned and led?

   _____

   _____

   b. Were any goals suggested or set before the students? If so, what were they?

   _____

   _____

   c. Was the teacher excited about and deeply involved in learning?

   _____

   _____

   d. Were any rewards used? If so, what were they?

   _____

   _____

   e. Was there any attempt to use assignments? If so, how?

   _____

   _____

   f. Did the teacher relate the lesson to the felt needs of the students? If so, what needs were appealed to?

   _____

   _____

   g. Were any divine appeals alluded to or touched on?
     Duty?_____
     Love? _____
     Reward?_____
     Fulfillment? _____
     Other?_____

h. Was the scriptural command to study and learn
brought to bear in any way?

_____

_____

8. Were any students led to Christ? Was there a prayer time,
a sense of real experience with Christ, during the class or
at its conclusion?

_____

_____

9. Was there a strong rapport between the class and the teacher?

_____

_____

10. What changes would you expect in the students' lives as
a result of the class session?

_____

_____

a. Was the main lesson idea adequately exposed?

_____

b. Was it repeated?

_____

c. Was it clear and understood?

_____

d. Was there a conviction accompanying the idea?

_____

e. Was there a sense of acceptance and desire to adapt
the lesson truth or idea?

_____

_____

11. In what ways were the basic principles leading to change brought into play?

   a. Beginning where the student is?

   _____

   _____

   b. Moving from the known to the unknown?

   _____

   _____

   c. Challenging the student to improve?

   _____

   d. Relating the lesson to student needs?

   _____

   _____

   e. Personal testimony or backing up of the lesson idea by the teacher?

   _____

12. What evidences were there of the teacher's involvement during the week in preparing the lesson, in relating to the students, and in participating in the total work of the church?

   _____

   _____

13. Summarize your experience in observation, including the things you have learned and the conclusions drawn.

   _____

   _____

14. Be prepared to discuss your experiences in class, highlighting your more significant observations.

   _____

   _____